$4.50

MORE HOUGEN FAVORITES

More Hougen Favorites

By
RICHARD T. HOUGEN

MORE HOUGEN FAVORITES
COPYRIGHT © 1971 BY RICHARD T. HOUGEN

Library of Congress Catalog Card Number: 71-149644

SET UP, PRINTED, AND BOUND BY THE
PARTHENON PRESS, AT NASHVILLE,
TENNESSEE, UNITED STATES OF AMERICA

TO MY
TWO GRAND-DAUGHTERS
CHRISTIANA AND CARY
MAY THEY CARRY ON THE TRADITION
OF GOOD COOKERY

THE ARTWORK

THE ORNAMENTAL BORDERS INTRODUCING THE VARIOUS FOOD SECTIONS AND THE COVER DESIGN ARE FINE LINE PEN AND INK DRAWINGS BY DONA CLARE HOUGEN MARSHALL, DAUGHTER OF THE AUTHOR. MRS. MARSHALL WAS BORN IN BEREA, KENTUCKY, GRADUATED FROM THE COLLEGE OF WILLIAM AND MARY AND NOW RESIDES WITH HER HUSBAND, PETER JAY MARSHALL, AND TWO DAUGHTERS, CHRISTIANA AND CARY IN WESTBORO, MASSACHUSETTS.

THE AUTHOR

RICHARD T. HOUGEN, ASSOCIATE PROFESSOR OF HOTEL MANAGEMENT AT BEREA COLLEGE AND MANAGER OF BOONE TAVERN HOTEL SINCE 1940, IS THE AUTHOR OF TWO OTHER COOKBOOKS . . . *LOOK NO FURTHER* AND *COOKING WITH HOUGEN*.

THE BOOK COMPOSITION

SET IN LYDIAN ROMAN AND CURSIVE TYPES
PRINTED ON INDIA BECKETT TEXT
THE PARTHENON PRESS
NASHVILLE, TENNESSEE

PREFACE

For those of us who like to eat we must have someone who likes to cook.

Today's shopping offers us shelf upon shelf of every dreamed of foodstuffs . . . in cans . . . frozen . . . freeze dried . . . pre-mixed . . . or heat and serve. We are fortunate to have these convenient foods for the career man or woman,

BUT

here is my third cookbook designed to interest, pique the curious, and excite the appetite.

Recipes to assist us in maintaining the heritage of good cooking, some reminiscent of years gone by, some foreign foods adapted to the American palate, and some unusual combinations.

The ingredients are familiar and usually on your kitchen shelf. The tested recipes are easy to read and easy to follow. The results will please you and your guests.

What more can I say than to tell you what one guest asked me after he had finished his dinner. . . . "Can I marry your cook?"

CONTENTS

Breakfast
Dishes

BAKED DOUGHNUTS

½ cup sugar
1 teaspoon nutmeg
½ teaspoon salt
1 egg, well beaten
2 tablespoons melted lard
2 cups sifted flour
3 teaspoons baking powder
½ cup milk

METHOD:

1. Mix sugar, nutmeg, and salt. Add the egg and mix well.
2. Add the lard and beat well.
3. Sift the flour with the baking powder.
4. Add the flour mixture with the milk alternately. Begin and end with some flour. Mix well.
5. Place dough on a floured pastry board and roll out to ¾ inch thickness. Cut with a doughnut cutter and place them on a well-greased baking sheet. Brush the tops of the doughnuts with some melted lard.
6. Bake at 425 F. for 8 minutes.
7. Coat the doughnuts with a generous amount of confectioners' sugar.

Yields 18 doughnuts.

This recipe is planned to eliminate the deep fat frying process. Place the coated doughnuts in an air-tight container to keep them from drying out.

GREAT DAY PANCAKES AND MUFFINS

1 cup flour, sift before measuring
½ cup white cornmeal
2½ teaspoons baking powder
2 tablespoons sugar
½ teaspoon salt
1 cup bran flakes (cereal)
1 cup buttermilk
¼ teaspoon baking soda
4 eggs, well beaten
3 tablespoons oleomargarine, melted

METHOD:

1. Sift flour, baking powder, salt, and sugar. Add the cornmeal and bran flakes and mix well.
2. Mix the soda with the buttermilk.
3. Add the buttermilk and eggs and beat together.
4. Add the oleomargarine and mix well.
5. Bake on a hot griddle, 375 F. When pancakes show bubbles on top turn cake and bake the other side.
6. Serve with hot maple or sugar syrup.

Yields 16 pancakes.

THIS BATTER CAN ALSO BE BAKED FOR MUFFINS. PLACE IN WELL-GREASED MUFFIN PAN AND BAKE AT 400 F. for 10 minutes, then INCREASE HEAT TO 450 F.

for 5 minutes. Allow to set a few minutes before loosening the muffin from the pan with a knife.

Yields 12 muffins.

HONEY BUTTER WHIP

½ pound butter
2½ cups confectioners' sugar
(powdered sugar)
1 cup honey

METHOD:

1. Place softened butter, sugar, and honey in an electric mixer. Beat at high speed until light and creamy.
2. Butter may be kept in the refrigerator until needed. Allow butter to come to room temperature before serving.

This amount should serve 18 . . . yield is 3 cups

Honey Butter is a tasty spread for hot biscuits, toast, English muffins, and pancakes.

KENTUCKY FRIED APPLES

2 medium sized tart cooking
apples, you will need 2 cups
½ to ¾ cup sugar
¼ cup oleomargarine

METHOD:

1. With your paring knife peel a 1½ inch strip around the center of the apple. This band will then remove about a third of the apple peel.
2. Cut the apple into quarters. Next slice each quarter into 3 or 4 sections as you would section an orange.
3. Place the apples, sugar, and oleomargarine in a very heavy skillet or cooking pan. Cover and place on a medium heat. When mixture begins to cook allow 10 minutes of cooking time.
4. Remove the cover and cook 5 or 10 minutes longer until apples are tender and rather transparent. You may need to reduce the heat to low during this final cooking stage. Should your apples be juiceless you may wish to add a small amount of water to give moisture.

Yields 3 servings.

Fried apples, sausage cakes, hominy grits, and biscuits make for good breakfast fare. In fact the fried apples taste so good at any meal. They are a bit difficult to make until you get the knack of it, but well worth the effort.

16

OMELET A LA NORMANDIE

2 eggs, room temperature
2 tablespoons oleomargarine

METHOD:

1. Beat the eggs with a wire whisk, a french balloon whip, fine wire type is best, until the eggs are thick and lemon colored, about 8 to 10 minutes. They will look almost like yellow whipped cream.
2. Heat an omelet pan to medium high heat or a bit hotter. Add the oleomargarine and when it has melted pour in the beaten eggs.
3. Lift the edges of the omelet to allow some of the egg to roll under the edges and cook.
4. When all the egg is about ⅘ percent cooked and remainder of the eggs are frothy remove the omelet to a plate. As you slide the omelet onto the plate, flip, using a spatula, the half over the bottom half, cooked side on top.
5. This will be a cooked omelet with a frothy center.

Yields 1 omelet.   THE ABSOLUTE IN OMELETS

NOTE: YOU CAN PREPARE ONLY ONE AT A TIME.

Oleomargarine used as butter tends to burn easily.

TEA TIME TOAST

4 slices white bread, trim
 crusts, cut diagonally
1 well beaten egg
⅓ cup milk
¼ cup granulated sugar
½ teaspoon cinnamon
½ cup confectioners' sugar

METHOD:

1. Add the milk to the egg and mix well.
2. Dip the pieces of bread into the mixture and fry
   in deep fat at 350 F. or in a skillet with oleomargine,
   about 2 tablespoons, adding more if needed.
3. Remove from the fat and toss in the cinnamon sugar
   and then coat each piece with the confectioners' sugar.

Yields 2 servings.

Excellent for tea or served with a fruit salad luncheon
or as a dessert served with preserves.

NOTES

NOTES

Soups

ASPARAGUS SOUP

6 tablespoons butter
4 tablespoons flour
3 cups milk
2 cups chicken stock
2 14½ ounce cans green
    asparagus (pureed),
    juice and all
½ teaspoon salt
¼ teaspoon pepper
¼ cup chopped parsley
Whipped cream for topping
of soup and dash of
ground mace.

METHOD:

1. Melt butter in top of double boiler. Add the flour and blend. Cook 4 minutes.
2. Add the milk and chicken stock. Blend and cook 12 minutes.
3. Add the pureed asparagus and juice. Mix and heat to boiling point.
4. Add salt, pepper, and parsley.
5. Serve with a dash of whipped cream on top of each cup of soup and just a sprinkling of mace on top of the cream.

Serves 12 to 14.

Serve either hot or cold.

BROCCOLI ROQUEFORT SOUP

3 cups chicken stock (could
use bouillon cubes)
1 pint of milk
¼ cup flour
2 tablespoons chicken fat
(could use butter)
2 cups cooked broccoli, use
chopped frozen type
¼ cup Roquefort cheese,
grated

METHOD:

1. Make a roux by cooking the flour with the chicken fat
two minutes, stirring continuously.
2. Add the chicken stock and milk. Cook 5 minutes.
3. Add the broccoli, which you have pureed. Add the
grated cheese.
4. Blend all together well.

Yields 6 servings.

CORN CHOWDER

4 cups chicken broth (fresh
or made from bouillon
cubes)
2 cups milk
2 tablespoons butter
½ a bay leaf
5 tablespoons flour
1 peppercorn
1 cup whole kernel corn
(Number 303 can yields
2 cups of corn)
liquid from canned corn
¾ cup
2 tablespoons oleomargarine
¼ teaspoon salt
¼ teaspoon pepper
½ cup diced fine celery
¼ cup diced fine green
pepper
1 tablespoon chopped
pimiento
2 tablespoons chopped fine
green onion tops
2 tablespoons chopped fine
cooked crisp bacon

METHOD:

1. Melt the butter, add the flour and cook as you
stir to make a roux. Cook about 4 minutes.

2. Combine the milk and stock, heat, add the roux and stir to prevent lumping. Cook for 15 minutes on simmer. Add the peppercorn and bayleaf.
3. Add the corn and corn liquid. Cook for 10 minutes.
4. Saute (pan fry in the oleomargarine) the celery, green pepper, salt, and pepper. Add to the stock mixture and simmer 20 minutes.
5. Remove the bayleaf and peppercorn. Add the pimiento, green onions, and bacon.

Yields 8 servings.

CREAM OF CHICKEN SOUP

4 cups chicken stock
(fresh or use bouillon cubes to make stock)
1 bay leaf
¼ teaspoon pepper
5 tablespoons flour
1 cup chicken stock
2 cups milk, scalded
¼ cup chopped onions
2 tablespoons oleomargarine
1 tablespoon chopped fine parsley
½ cup fine cut cooked chicken

METHOD:

1. Heat the 4 cups of stock, bay leaf, and pepper. Simmer 10 minutes.
2. Mix the flour with the cup of broth and add to the stock. Stir to prevent lumping and simmer 10 minutes.
3. Add the hot milk and simmer 10 minutes.
4. Saute (pan fry) the onions in the oleomargarine and add to the soup. Simmer 10 minutes.
5. Remove the bay leaf and add the parsley and cut chicken.

Yields 8 servings.

CREAM OF CHICKEN GIBLET

Soup may be made by adding ¼ cup of fine cut celery and ½ cup fine cut cooked chicken giblets which you saute with the onions in step number 4.

CREAM OF PARSLEY SOUP

1 pint chicken stock
1 pint milk
⅓ cup flour
3 tablespoons butter
¼ teaspoon salt
⅛ teaspoon pepper
1 cup chopped parsley
2 tablespoons butter
¼ cup finely chopped onion

27

METHOD:

1. Make roux of flour and 3 tablespoons butter.
2. Mix and cook roux, chicken stock, milk, salt, and pepper for 20-30 minutes.
3. Saute parsley and onion in 2 tablespoons butter. Add to soup.
4. Serve sprinkled with freshly grated nutmeg.

Serves 4 to 6.

FRENCH ONION SOUP

1 cup onions, chopped
¼ cup oleomargarine
¼ cup flour
1 cup sliced onions (thinly)
¼ teaspoon pepper
¼ teaspoon celery seed
1 bay leaf (remove before serving)
1 quart beef stock
1 pint chicken stock
¼ cup finely cut green onion
¼ cup finely cut green onion tops
Bread croutons and Parmesan Cheese

METHOD:

1. Saute (pan fry) the chopped onions in the oleo-margarine.

28

2. Add the flour and stir to blend.
3. Add the cup of finely sliced onions, pepper, celery seed, bay leaf and stocks.
4. Simmer on medium heat for 20 minutes.
5. Add the green onion tops and bottoms.
6. Serve with a toast crouton on top of the soup. Sprinkle generously with Parmesan cheese.

Serves 8.

RICELAND SOUP

2 quarts chicken stock
1 quart cooked rice, pureed
2 cups tomato juice
⅛ teaspoon celery salt
⅛ teaspoon ground thyme
⅛ teaspoon ground bay leaf
¼ teaspoon pepper

METHOD:

1. Cook all together, simmer for 30 minutes.

Serves 12.

SPLIT PEA SOUP, ST. GERMAINE

1 cup green split peas
¾ quart water
1½ quarts water
1 pint chicken stock
½ bay leaf
¾ teaspoon chopped dried
   mint leaves
¼ teaspoon thyme
½ teaspoon salt
¼ teaspoon pepper
¼ cup flour
2 tablespoons chicken fat
   or butter
¼ cup chopped cooked crisp
   bacon
¼ cup finely chopped
   cooked ham
3 tablespoons finely
   chopped parsley
½ cup finely cut green
   onions (tops and all)
   croutons

METHOD:

1. Soak peas overnight in ¾ quart water.
2. Drain peas. Cook them in 1½ quarts water and the
chicken stock.
3. Add bay leaf, mint, thyme, salt, and pepper.

4. When peas are tender, remove bay leaf.
5. Add roux made by cooking flour and fat. Stir and cook to thicken somewhat. Remove from heat.
6. Add bacon, ham, parsley, and onions.
7. Season further to taste.
8. Serve with croutons.

Yields 2 quarts, 8 servings.

SOUTHERN PEANUT SOUP

1 cup finely chopped cooked ham
2 cups fine cut green onions (1 cup of onion and 1 cup of the green tops)
½ cup oleomargarine
1 cup sifted flour
2 cups unsalted peanuts, blanched, chopped very fine
1½ quarts chicken stock, you could use 2 bouillon cubes per cup of hot water
1 quart beef stock, bouillon cubes could be used also

METHOD:

1. Saute (pan fry) the ham, peanuts, and white onion in the oleomargarine.

2. Add the flour. Blend and cook 4 minutes. Stir to prevent sticking.
3. Add the soup stocks. Blend with a wire whip and cook for 15 minutes. Stir occasionally.
4. Just before serving add the onion tops and simmer 10 minutes.

Yields 16 servings.

If you use blanched salted peanuts wash the peanuts in hot water to remove the salt.

NOTES

NOTES

Meats
Poultry
AND
ACCOMPANIMENTS

BAKED CHICKEN COUNTRY INN

4 legs and 4 breasts of
  chicken (fryers)
  (butter to rub chicken)
1 teaspoon ground thyme
1 teaspoon tarragon leaves
  (crushed)
5 cups chicken broth
½ cup butter
1 cup flour
8 ounces canned mushrooms
¼ teaspoon salt
⅛ teaspoon pepper

METHOD:

1. Rub the chicken with butter and sprinkle well with the thyme and tarragon.
2. Place in a buttered baking pan. Pour chicken broth over the chicken and cover. Bake at 375 F. for 1½ hours.
3. Place the butter in top of double boiler and add the flour. Stir and cook for 5 minutes. Add 6 cups of the drippings from the baked chicken and the drained juice from the mushrooms. Cook until thickened and then pour the sauce back over the chicken and sprinkle the mushrooms over the top.
4. Cover and bake at 400 F. for 1 hour.
5. Serve with Poppyseed Noodles or Bread Dumplings.

Serves 6-8.

BAKED VEAL MINCE TANQUERVILLE

1 pound ground veal
½ cup cracker crumbs
1 teaspoon salt
½ teaspoon pepper
½ teaspoon thyme
1 cup milk
1 egg
5 strips of bacon
1¾ cups coffee cream
1¾ cups milk

METHOD:

1. Mix the first 7 ingredients together well.
2. Shape into 5 patties. Wrap each with a slice of bacon and secure the bacon with a toothpick.
3. Place in a small roasting pan or casserole, cover, and bake for 1 hour at 325 F.
4. Remove the patties and stir 4 tablespoons of flour into the milk to make a smooth mixture. Add the cream to the milk. Mix this into the drippings remaining in the roaster. Add ½ teaspoon of salt and ½ teaspoon of pepper. Stir well to prevent lumping of the sauce.
5. Place the patties back into the roaster and pour the sauce over the meat. Cover and bake at 325 F. for 1 hour.
6. Serve each patty with some of the sauce over each and a garnish of fresh parsley.

Yields 5 servings.

Should your sauce curdle you may place the sauce in a bowl and beat with a rotary egg beater to smooth the sauce. Then serve the sauce over the meat.

BASIC DRESSING TO SERVE WITH MEATS

1½ cups cornbread broken in pieces
1 cup white bread, stale, broken in pieces
½ tablespoon leaf sage, crumbled up (could use ground sage, though not as tasty)
⅛ teaspoon black pepper
1 cup rich chicken stock (could use 2 chicken bouillon cubes dissolved in hot water)
¼ cup minced fine onions

METHOD:

1. Mix all together.
2. Place in a greased baking pan and bake at 350 F. for 35 minutes.

Yields 5-6 servings.

CRANBERRY DRESSING

METHOD:

1. Use above recipe cutting down to ⅛ cup onion and ⅛ teaspoon sage.
2. Add 1 cup chopped (coarsely) fresh cranberries.

Yields 5-6 servings of a tart dressing.

MINT DRESSING

METHOD:

1. Add to Basic Dressing Recipe:
   ¼ cup chopped fine fresh mint leaves (could use dried mint).
   ⅛ cup chopped fine parsley.

Yields 5-6 servings.

BREAD DUMPLINGS

2 cups bread crumbs
(made by breaking up
bread or rolls into
small pieces)
½ cup flour
1½ teaspoons baking powder
¼ teaspoon salt
¼ teaspoon onion salt
⅛ teaspoon celery salt
¼ cup finely cut green
onion tops
1 well-beaten egg
½ cup milk

METHOD:

1. Sift together flour, baking powder, and salts.
2. Mix with bread crumbs.
3. Add onions.
4. Add milk to egg. Stir into dry mixture.
5. Shape dumplings with the hands into balls the size of a golf ball.
6. Place in steamer and steam 15 minutes.

Yields 14 dumplings.

A steamer may be improvised by using a kettle of boiling water over which you place a collander, be sure the bottom of the collander does not touch the water. Grease the sides and bottom of the collander and place your dumplings in here.

BREAST OF CHICKEN INDIENNE, FRUITED RICE

4 chicken breasts (2 pounds)
salt and pepper
5½ cups chicken broth
1½ teaspoon curry powder
½ cup oleomargarine
¾ cup flour

METHOD:

1. Salt and pepper the chicken breasts.
2. Melt the oleomargarine in the top of a double boiler. Add the flour and mix. Cook, stirring, for a few minutes.
3. Add the stock, reserve about ¼ cup of the stock to moisten the curry powder.
4. Cook the stock and roux for 8 minutes. Stir to prevent lumping. Add the moistened curry powder, salt and pepper to taste. Blend the sauce together.
5. Place the chicken breasts in a buttered casserole and pour the sauce over the chicken. Bake at 350 F. for 2 hours.

FRUITED RICE

3 cups boiled rice
¼ cup seeded raisins
¼ cup currants
¼ cup sour red cherries, cut
in pieces
⅛ cup melted butter
(2 tablespoons)
salt to taste

METHOD:

A. Mix the hot rice with the fruits and butter.
B. Serve a piece of chicken over a mound of the rice and
the Curry Sauce from the casserole over the top of
each piece of chicken.

Serves 4.

NOTE THAT YOU MAY USE SLICES OF ROASTED
TURKEY HEATED IN SOME TURKEY BROTH IN PLACE
OF THE CHICKEN BREASTS. IN THIS CASE YOU WOULD
ONLY COOK THE SAUCE AND HEAT THE TURKEY. YOU
WOULD NOT BAKE THE TURKEY.

BEEF CUBELETTES OLYMPIA

1 pound beef sirloin cut into
1-inch cubes
3 tablespoons flour
¼ to ½ teaspoon black pepper
(depends on how peppery
you like it)
¼ teaspoon salt
4 tablespoons butter
(oleomargarine is easier to
brown meat in)
½ cup sliced meat from black
olives
½ cup cut mushrooms
¼ cup mushroom liquid
1 cup beef bouillon
(could use 2 bouillon
cubes per cup water)

METHOD:
1. Mix flour, salt, and pepper.
2. Toss the cubes of meat into the flour mixture and lightly coat the meat.
3. Brown meat in butter.
4. Remove the meat and add the beef stock. Stir to prevent mixture lumping and cook for 5 minutes.
5. Add the mushrooms, juice of mushrooms, and olives. Mix. Add the meat cubes and stir together.
6. Bake in a casserole, covered, for 2 hours at 350 F.
7. Serve from the casserole or on toast points.

Yields 4 to 5 servings.

CINNAMON BERRY JELLY

¾ cup water
¼ cup lemon juice
2 cups apple juice
8 whole cloves
¼ teaspoon mace
½ cup cinnamon imperials
(red hots)
1 cinnamon stick
1 box Surejell or other fruit
pectin for jelly making
1 teaspoon red food coloring
4 cups sugar

METHOD:

1. Mix the first 9 ingredients and bring to a rolling boil.
2. Add the sugar and stir. Bring to a rolling boil and cook 2 minutes.
3. Pour into 4 eight-ounce jelly glasses and let stand over night to set.

Excellent with meat and chicken dishes.

ITALIAN SPAGHETTI

   1½ pounds ground beef
   ½ pound ground pork
   2 medium sized Italian onions (purple skin), chopped
   2 green peppers, chopped fine
   2 cloves of garlic
   ½ teaspoon salt
   ½ teaspoon ground thyme
   ¼ teaspoon celery salt
   ¼ teaspoon pepper
   ¼ teaspoon oregano leaves (crushed)
   2 six ounce cans tomato paste
   2 one-pound 12-ounce cans tomatoes
   1 6-ounce can mushrooms (pieces and stems)
   1 14-ounce box spaghetti
   Parmesan Cheese

METHOD:

1. Brown the first 5 ingredients in skillet with 2 ounces olive oil.
2. Add the next 5 seasonings and 1 can of tomato paste and 1 can of tomatoes.

3. Mix well and place in a 350 F. oven for 1 hour. Stir occasionally.
4. Next add the other can of tomato paste and tomatoes. Add also the can of mushrooms and liquid. Bake another hour, stirring occasionally.
5. Remove from the oven and cover with aluminum foil or air tight cover and bake for another hour at 375 F.
6. Cook the spaghetti as directed on the package. Rinse and drain well. Then add butter to coat the spaghetti nicely.
7. Serve a mound of spaghetti with a generous serving of the sauce and sprinkle with Parmesan Cheese.

Serves 6 generously.

MEDALLIONS OF PORK

16 pork chops, center cut, ¼ inch thick, 1½ pounds trimmed
6 tablespoons oleomargarine
½ tablespoon salt
½ tablespoon pepper
1 teaspoon chopped parsley
½ teaspoon chopped chives
½ teaspoon pulverized rosemary leaves
½ teaspoon Summer Savory
2 cups apple juice mixed with 4 tablespoons cornstarch
½ cup water

METHOD:

1. Trim fat and bone from each chop, forming the medallions.
2. Mix all the seasonings with the oleomargarine. Place this mixture in a skillet and add the medallions.
3. Brown the meat lightly using not too high a heat.
4. Remove the meat and add the apple juice mixture. Cook for 5 minutes, stir to prevent lumping. Add the water and mix.
5. Place the meat in a casserole and pour the sauce over the medallions. Bake at 375 F. for 2 hours, covered.
6. Serve 3 or 4 medallions on buttered egg noodles and pour some of the sauce over the meat.

Yields 4 to 5 servings.

MINCED CHICKEN OR TURKEY PATTY

4 cups minced chicken or turkey, cooked
1 cup chicken cream sauce
2 eggs, beaten
½ teaspoon salt
¼ teaspoon pepper

METHOD:

1. Mix ingredients together.
2. Shape in 5-ounce patties and grill in small amount of butter.
3. Serve with sauce.

Yields 8 servings.

CHICKEN CREAM SAUCE

3 cups chicken stock
½ cup flour
¼ cup butter

METHOD:

1. Heat stock.
2. Thicken with roux made of the flour and butter.

Serves 8.

MINT JELLY

1 cup vinegar
2 tablespoons dried or
chopped fresh mint leaves
2 cups water
1 box Sure Jell or equivalent
jelly-making pectin
4 cups sugar
¼ teaspoon green food
coloring

METHOD:

1. Mix vinegar, water, Sure Jell, and mint leaves. Stir and
bring to a boil.
2. Add sugar, stir well, bring to a rolling boil and cook
3 minutes.

3. Add green food coloring.
4. Pour into jelly glasses and let stand several hours to set.

Yields four 8-ounce glasses of jelly.

Delightful with Roast Leg of Lamb or Broiled Lamb Chops.

PLANTATION HAM

1 8-pound ham
1 cup brown sugar
½ cup prepared mustard
½ teaspoon allspice

METHOD:
1. Mix the ingredients and spread over the ham.
2. Bake covered for 2½ hours at 350 F.

SAUCE

1 cup apple cider
4 tablespoons cornstarch
½ cup orange juice
½ cup sugar
½ cup vinegar
1 cup currants
1 cup orange marmalade
1 cup drippings from the baked ham

METHOD:

1. Mix cider, orange juice, vinegar, sugar, and cornstarch.
2. Cook in the top of a double boiler for 5 minutes to thicken.
3. Add the currants, marmalade, and drippings. Serve the sauce over the slices of baked ham.

   8 pound (bone in) ham serves 14 to 16, boneless serves 20-24.

PORK CHOPS, AUSTRIAN STYLE

pork chops
thyme
pepper
tarragon
salt
chicken broth
flour
canned mushrooms

METHOD:

1. Trim fat from chops, place them in baking pan.
2. Sprinkle seasonings (⅛ teaspoon of each, per chop) over chops. Pour chicken broth (¼ cup, per chop) over chops. Bake at 375 F. for 1½ hours covered.
3. Remove from oven. Pour off liquid, measure it. For every cup of liquid add 2 tablespoons of flour mixed with 2 tablespoons cold water.
4. Put 1½ tablespoons mushrooms over each chop. Pour mushroom liquid into the gravy.
5. Pour gravy over chops, place again in 375 F. oven, covered, and cook for 1½ hours. Serve each chop with a bread dumpling and some of the gravy. Be sure the gravy goes on the dumpling, too.

ROAST LEG OF VEAL OREGANO

A veal roast from leg, 4 or
5 pounds
½ cup oleomargarine
½ cup flour
2 teaspoons oregano
2 teaspoons caraway seed
2 tablespoons salt
1 teaspoon pepper
2 oranges thinly sliced
1 cup orange juice

GRAVY

6 tablespoons flour
4 tablespoons water

METHOD:

1. Rub the meat with the oleomargarine. Sift the flour with the spices and sprinkle over the meat.
2. Place the meat in a roaster and place the orange slices over the top of the meat. Pour the orange juice in the bottom of the pan.
3. Cover and bake at 350 F. for 2 hours. Bake 1 more hour uncovered.
4. Add 4 cups of water and bake for 1½ hours.
5. Drain off the juices. Mix the flour and water to a smooth paste and add to the juices and cook until thickened.

Serve the sliced meat on a mound of the following dressing and a serving of the gravy.

DRESSING

> 4 cups cornbread, broken in pieces
> 4 cups broken rolls or white bread
> ½ cup chopped onions which have been sauteed (pan fried) in ½ cup of chicken fat or oleomargarine.
> ½ teaspoon pepper
> 1½ teaspoons oregano
> 2½ cups chicken broth (could use bouillon cubes mixed with water)

METHOD:

A. Mix bread with onion and seasonings. Add the broth and mix together. Place in a greased baking pan and bake at 375 F. for 1 hour.

A 4 pound roast should serve 8 to 12 people.

SAVORY VEAL STEAK

4-6 veal steaks, ½ inch thick
1 teaspoon flour per steak
½ teaspoon salt per steak
¼ teaspoon pepper per steak
⅛ teaspoon savory
per steak
3 tablespoons butter
¼ cup water
1 tablespoon flour
1 cup sour cream

METHOD:

1. Sprinkle each side of steaks with mixture of flour, salt, pepper, and savory.
2. Saute in butter to brown, at rather high heat.
3. Remove meat, add water mixed with 1 tablespoon flour. Stir well, cook for 5 minutes.
4. Add sour cream and mix.
5. Pour sauce over steaks and bake covered at 350 F. for 1½ hours.

Serves 4-6.

SIRLOIN OF BEEF TISZANO

2 pounds of beef sirloin,
cut in 1-inch cubes
½ cup green pepper, cut in
thin strips
1 cup sliced mushrooms
plus the liquid (canned
mushrooms)
½ cup flour
1 teaspoon salt
½ teaspoon pepper
⅛ cup freeze-dried chives
½ cup oleomargarine
2 cups sour cream
1½ cups chicken stock (fresh
or made from bouillon
cubes)

METHOD:

1. Mix the flour with the salt and pepper.
2. Toss the beef cubes into the flour mixture to coat each
   cube.
3. Brown the meat in a skillet with the oleomargarine, at
   high heat. Remove the meat.
4. Reduce the heat and add the chicken stock and the
   mushroom liquid (½ cup) to the drippings in the pan.
5. Cook for 5 minutes to thicken mixture slightly.
6. Remove from the fire and add the remaining ingredients.

7. Combine gravy mixture with the meat.
8. Bake, covered, at 375 F. for 1 hour and 45 minutes.
9. Serve in the casserole or on toast points.

Yields 8 servings.

STAFFORDSHIRE SAUCE

¼ cup bread crumbs
1 cup sour cream
¼ cup horseradish (use less
   if milder sauce desired)
salt
pepper

METHOD:

1. Blend ingredients.
2. Salt and pepper to taste.

Serves 6.

Excellent served with Roast Leg of Mutton or Lamb.

STEAK VALENCIA

1½ pounds round steak, 6 steaks cut ¾ inch thick
12 teaspoons flour
½ teaspoon pepper
1 teaspoon salt
3 tablespoons oleomargarine
1 cup water
½ cup chopped onions
¼ cup sweet pickle relish
2 medium-sized tomatoes cut in sections, as you would an orange
½ green pepper cut into ⅛ inch thick strips, 1½ inches long
1½ tablespoons flour mixed in 3 tablespoons water

METHOD:

1. Sprinkle each side of each steak with some of the flour, pepper, and salt which has been mixed together.
2. Place the oleomargarine in the bottom of a baking dish or dutch oven and place the steaks on top. Bake at 400 F. for 30 minutes. Add the water to the meat and bake 30 minutes.
3. Spread the pickle relish, onions, green pepper strips and tomato wedges over the top of the steaks.

4. Cover the meat and bake for 45 minutes.
5. Remove the steak from the baking dish and add the flour and water mixture to the drippings. Stir well to prevent lumping and cook for 5 minutes.
6. Serve some of the gravy underneath each steak.

Yields 6 servings.

STUFFED LAMB CHOPS MAHARAJAH

8 lamb chops, 5 ounces each, trim off the fat
½ cup fine cut cooked ham
½ cup currants, soak in ½ cup warm water for ½ hour
1 beaten egg
2 cups fine bread crumbs, crumbled by hand
3½ cups apple juice
1 tablespoon curry powder
3 tablespoons flour

METHOD:

1. Mix the currants, ham, egg, bread crumbs, and ½ cup apple juice.
2. Split the chop to form a pocket and stuff each with some of the dressing. Secure shut by using a toothpick.
3. Brown the chops lightly in 4 tablespoons oleomargarine.
4. Remove the chops to a casserole. Add 3 cups apple juice which you have blended with the flour. Cook, stirring to prevent lumping. Add ½ teaspoon salt and ¼ teaspoon pepper. Mix together. Add the curry powder mixed with ½ cup apple juice.
5. Pour the sauce over the chops and bake, covered, at 375 F. for 1½ hours.
6. Serve 2 chops to an order with the sauce over the chops.

Yields 4 servings.

SWISS STEAK IN DILL SAUCE

4 swiss steaks, cut from top round of beef, 6 ounces each
1 teaspoon salt
2 cups water
2 tablespoons flour
2 teaspoons dill seeds
6 tablespoons oleomargarine
¼ teaspoon pepper
½ teaspoon salt

METHOD:

1. Sprinkle ½ teaspoon of salt on each steak, some on each side.
2. Saute (pan fry) the steaks in the 6 tablespoons of oleomargarine.
3. Remove steaks to a baking pan.
4. Mix the water with the flour to form a smooth paste. Add to the drippings in the pan in which the steaks were sauteed. Stir to prevent lumping and cook until mixture thickens.
5. Add the dill seeds, the ¼ teaspoon pepper and ½ teaspoon of salt. Pour gravy over the steaks.
6. Cover the meat and bake at 375 F. for 1½ to 2 hours.
7. Serve the meat with a portion of the gravy over one part of each steak.

Yields 4 servings.

VEAL CHOPS PERUGINA

6 veal chops, cut ¾ inch thick
3 tablespoons butter
2 tablespoons flour
¼ teaspoon salt
¼ teaspoon pepper
½ teaspoon basil
2 cups chicken broth
1 pint tomatoes
4 cups cooked macaroni (7 ounces raw, cooked in 2 quarts boiling water with ¾ teaspoon salt; cook as directed on package)
½ cup butter
¼ teaspoon pepper
1 cup grated yellow cheese

METHOD:

1. Brown veal chops in 3 tablespoons butter. Remove from skillet. Add flour, ¼ teaspoon salt, ¼ teaspoon pepper, and basil. Cook 1 minute.
2. Add broth and mix well. Add tomatoes and blend.
3. Pour over meat. Cover and bake 375 F. for 1½ hours.
4. Remove chops and thicken sauce by adding 2 tablespoons flour mixed with ¼ cup water and cook to thicken about 5 minutes.
5. Serve chops on macaroni mixed with ½ cup butter,

½ teaspoon salt, ¼ teaspoon pepper, and cheese. Pour ¼ cup of gravy over edge of each chop.

Serves 6.

NOTES

NOTES

NOTES

Vegetables
and
Potatoes

ASPARAGUS PUDDING

1 pint thick cream sauce
salt
pepper
3 well-beaten egg yolks
2 cups cut-up cooked asparagus
3 stiffly beaten egg whites

METHOD:

1. Salt and pepper cream sauce to taste.
2. Add egg yolks. Cook in double boiler 4 minutes.
3. Add asparagus.
4. Fold in egg whites.
5. Bake in two well buttered casseroles in water bath 35-50 minutes at 350 F.

Serves 12-15.

Water bath—place the casseroles in a pan in which you place water about 1 inch deep . . . this will keep the custard from curdling.

BAKED DUMPLINGS

2 cups flour, sift before measuring
1 cup coffee cream
¼ teaspoon baking soda mixed in ¼ cup buttermilk
5 teaspoons baking powder
2 eggs, well beaten
¾ teaspoon salt

METHOD:

1. Sift flour, baking powder, and salt.
2. Add the eggs, cream, buttermilk, and soda.
3. Mix well and drop 2 tablespoonfuls for each dumpling onto a well-greased baking pan.
4. Cover tightly so that no air can escape or enter. Aluminum foil will do nicely for this cover.
5. Bake at 400 F. for 15 minutes.

Yields about 14-16 dumplings.

A good short method to achieve a light dumpling without using a steaming process.

BAKED POTATO WITH WHIPPED HERB BUTTER

6 baked potatoes
4 tablespoons butter
pinch of pepper
pinch of salt
⅛ teaspoon celery seed
⅛ teaspoon garlic salt
¹⁄₁₆ teaspoon oregano

METHOD:

1. Soften butter and then whip with a fork or spoon until light and fluffy.
2. Add the seasonings and beat together.
3. Gash the baked potato across the top to make an X. Push the potato, using both hands, from the base. This will open the top, petal fashion.
4. Serve the herb butter in the opening.

Yields 6 servings.

CABBAGE AU GRATIN

1 quart of raw shredded cabbage
¾ cup water
½ teaspoon salt
2 cups medium thick
   cream sauce, page 74
⅔ cup grated American
   cheese
1 slice of bread cut into
   very tiny cubes
3 tablespoons melted butter

METHOD:

1. Place the cabbage in the boiling salted water. Cook until the cabbage has wilted down, about 5 minutes.
2. Mix ⅓ cup of cheese with the cream sauce. Add the cabbage. Mix and place in a well-greased casserole.
3. Distribute the other ⅓ cup of grated cheese over the top of the cabbage. Sprinkle the bread crumbs which have been mixed with the melted butter over the top of the cheese.
4. Bake at 400 F. for 30 minutes.

Yields 8 servings.

CORN, TOMATO, AND RICE CASSEROLE

1 cup corn, cut off the cob (or frozen corn)
1 cup chicken stock
1 cup fresh tomatoes, cut up into pieces
½ cup uncooked rice (quick type)
½ teaspoon salt
¼ teaspoon pepper
¼ teaspoon whole dill seeds
¼ teaspoon celery salt

METHOD:

1. Mix all ingredients together and place in well-greased casserole. Bake, covered, at 375 F. for 45 minutes to 1 hour.

Serves 6-8.

CREAM SAUCE

2 tablespoons butter
2 tablespoons sifted flour
½ teaspoon salt
¼ teaspoon pepper
1 cup hot milk

METHOD:

1. Melt butter in top of a double boiler.
2. Add the flour and stir with wire whip. Cook for 3 minutes.
3. Add the salt and pepper.
4. Add the hot milk. Stir and cook until thick and smooth. About 5 minutes.

This is a THICK CREAM SAUCE. For a MEDIUM THICK SAUCE use ¼ cup more milk. For a THIN SAUCE ½ cup more milk.

Yields 1 cup cream sauce.

CUSTARD POTATOES

3 potatoes, peeled, thinly sliced
1 teaspoon salt
¼ teaspoon pepper
1 teaspoon freeze dried chives
1 cup grated yellow American cheese
3 eggs, lightly beaten
1½ cups milk

METHOD:

1. Layer potatoes in greased casserole.
2. Sprinkle each layer with salt, pepper, chives, and cheese. Make 4 layers.
3. Mix eggs and milk together. Pour over potatoes.
4. Bake covered for 45 minutes at 350 F. Bake, uncovered 45 more minutes.

Serves 4-6.

DOUBLE BAKED POTATOES

4 medium-sized Idaho
    baking potatoes
½ cup hot milk
2 tablespoons butter
¼ teaspoon salt
⅛ teaspoon pepper
1 tablespoon chopped parsley

METHOD:
1. Rub the potatoes well with bacon fat, pierce with a fork to allow the steam to escape and bake at 375 F. for 1 to 1½ hours until tender.
2. Cut the potatoes in half lengthwise and remove the inside with the aid of a spoon.
3. Whip the potatoes and add the hot milk, butter, seasonings, and parsley. You may need to add more or less of the hot milk to make a fluffy potato.
4. Pile the potato back into the shells and sprinkle the tops with paprika.
5. Return the potatoes to a 400 F. oven to reheat.

Yields 6 to 8 filled halves.

EGGPLANT FRITTERS

1 cup eggplant, cut into ⅛ inch cubes

2 eggs, well beaten

2 tablespoons finely chopped onion

METHOD:

1. Peel eggplant. Cut into cubes and soak in salt water one hour.
2. Boil in fresh salted water until tender. Use ¼ cup water per cup of eggplant.
3. Drain the eggplant.
4. Add the eggs and onion. Mix well.
5. Fry as you would for pancakes on a griddle or in greased skillet.

Yields 9 fritters.

Serve as a vegetable or meat accompaniment.

ESCALLOPED OKRA

1 cup medium cream sauce
3 tablespoons melted butter
⅛ teaspoon salt
1½ cups drained canned okra
(number 303 size can)

METHOD:

1. Prepare cream sauce. Add melted butter.
2. Add salt.
3. Fold in okra. Take care not to break up the cut pieces of the vegetable.
4. Place in a buttered casserole.
5. Sprinkle top with fine bread crumbs.
6. Bake at 400 F. for 20 to 25 minutes.

Serves 4. If used with another vegetable this amount will serve 6.

A very easy vegetable dish to prepare. Most guests will believe it is asparagus. Don't tell, until you have an okra convert.

FRESH STRING BEANS PARMESAN

2 cups fresh cooked string
beans or seasoned
canned beans
⅓ cup grated Parmesan
cheese

METHOD:

1. Heat beans.
2. Fold cheese into beans. Add salt and pepper to taste.
Serve immediately.

Serves 4.

COOKING CANNED STRING BEANS

1 can string beans (about
2 cups)
¼ cup butter

METHOD:

1. Drain off half the liquid from the canned beans.
2. Place the beans and remaining liquid on to heat.
3. Add ¼ cup butter and salt and pepper to taste.
4. Cook at medium heat until the liquid is reduced.

Cook uncovered, of course, thus permiting the seasonings and butter to cook into the beans.

Serves 4.

GEORGIAN SWEET POTATOES

10 medium sweet potatoes,
fresh cooked or canned
⅛ cup butter
½ cup sorghum molasses,
New Orleans type mo-
lasses can be used for a
darker molasses flavor

METHOD:

1. Place the sliced sweet potatoes in a well-buttered baking dish or casserole.
2. Dot the tops of the potatoes with bits of the butter.
3. Pour the molasses over the tops of the potatoes.
4. Bake at 400 F. for 30 minutes.
5. Serve with some of the sauce over the potatoes.

Yields 6 servings.

HOLLANDAISE SAUCE

2 egg yolks, well beaten
1 teaspoon cornstarch
½ cup water
¼ pound butter
Juice of 1 lemon
dash of salt and pepper

METHOD:

1. Mix the cornstarch into the beaten egg yolks. Place in the top of a double boiler and add the water. Cook at not too high a heat and stir to prevent lumping.
2. When sauce has thickened add the butter and mix well. Add the lemon juice as you beat the sauce with a rotary egg beater. Add the salt and pepper.
3. The sauce is now ready for serving or you may cover and remove from the heat, reheating the sauce just before needed.

Serves 6.

This sauce is excellent for use over broccoli, asparagus, or cooked greens such as spinach, mustard, or kale.

MINTY FRESH CARROTS

1 pound carrots, sliced ¼ inch thick
½ cup oleomargarine
½ teaspoon finely chopped mint leaves (fresh or dried)
1 teaspoon salt
¼ teaspoon pepper

METHOD:

1. Cook carrots in boiling salted water. When tender, but not too soft, drain.
2. Add remaining ingredients. Cook for 3 minutes to blend seasonings.

Serves 4-6.

ONIONS IN CREAM

1 can of whole small onions, 15½ ounce-size can
2 cups medium thick cream sauce, page 74
½ teaspoon pepper
½ cup bread crumbs which have been buttered with 2 tablespoons melted butter paprika

METHOD:

1. Prepare the cream sauce.
2. Add the pepper and the drained onions. Mix together.
3. Place onions and sauce in well-buttered casserole.
4. Sprinkle the bread crumbs over the top of onions.
5. Sprinkle paprika over the top of the crumbs to give a colorful tone.
6. Bake at 350 F. at 30 minutes.

Yields 6 servings.

PINEAPPLE SWEET POTATOES

3 medium-sized sweet potatoes
¼ cup pineapple juice
2 tablespoons butter
½ cup drained crushed pineapple
¼ cup brown sugar
¼ teaspoon salt
½ cup shredded coconut
1 tablespoon white sugar

METHOD:

1. Boil the potatoes. Drain and whip, adding the pineapple juice and butter.
2. Add crushed pineapple, sugar, salt, and coconut. Mix.
3. Place in a well-covered casserole and bake at 375 F. for 30-40 minutes. Sprinkle with the white sugar and broil for a few minutes to brown the top of the potatoes.

Yields 6-8 servings.

PIQUANT POTATOES

2 medium sized potatoes,
  sliced thin
¼ cup radishes, sliced thin
1 tablespoon green pepper,
  cut fine
¼ cup oleomargarine
¼ cup water
  salt and pepper

METHOD:

1. Butter a casserole and place a layer of potatoes, a layer of radishes, salt and pepper, and then sprinkle some of the green pepper over the potatoes. Repeat this procedure.
2. Dot the top with the oleomargarine.
3. Pour the water over the mixture. Cover with a lid or foil.
4. Bake at 350 F. for 1 hour or until potatoes are tender.

Yields 4 servings.

SCALLOPED CHEESE

3 slices bread, well buttered
2 eggs, well beaten
¼ pound grated Cheddar Cheese
2 cups milk
¼ teaspoon salt
¼ teaspoon pepper

METHOD:

1. Place the bread in a buttered baking pan or casserole. Sprinkle cheese over tops of bread.
2. Mix the eggs, milk, salt, and pepper.
3. Pour liquid over the bread.
4. Bake, uncovered, for 50 minutes at 300 F.

This would make a pleasant luncheon dish served with Spanish Sauce or simply served with a dinner as an accompaniment dish.

Serves 4 to 6.

SAUERKRAUT SOUFFLE

3 tablespoons butter
1 teaspoon cornstarch
1 cup milk
3 beaten egg yolks
¼ teaspoon salt
⅛ teaspoon pepper
1 cup chopped fine sauerkraut
2 tablespoons chopped parsley
3 egg whites, beaten until stiff

METHOD:

1. Melt the butter in top of double boiler.
2. Add cornstarch and blend.
3. Add milk and blend.
4. Cook until thickened.
5. Add egg yolks, blend, and cook 2 minutes.
6. Add seasonings. Taste and add more if desired.
7. Add the chopped sauerkraut.
8. Add the chopped parsley. Blend all together.
9. Fold in the beaten egg whites.
10. Pour into a well-buttered casserole.
11. Top with fine bread crumbs. Bake at 350 F. for 30 minutes.

Yields 6 servings.

Delectable and different. No one will recognize the sauerkraut in this souffle.

VEGETABLES WITH DILL

1 cup cooked sliced carrots
1 cup fine-cut celery
2 tablespoons oleomargarine
2 tablespoons water
1 cup cooked frozen peas
1 teaspoon salt
½ teaspoon pepper
¾ teaspoon dill seeds
¼ cup oleomargarine

METHOD:

1. Saute (pan fry) the celery with the water and 2 table-spoons oleomargarine.
2. Mix all the other ingredients with the celery and bring to a well-heated stage before serving.

Yields 6 servings.

NOTES

NOTES

Salads

AMBROSIA SALAD

1 package lemon gelatin dessert powder
1 one pound can of white grapes (drain and measure juice and add enough apple juice to make 1¾ cups juice)
¼ cup vinegar
½ cup coconut
½ cup fine-cut celery
½ cup raisins
½ cup mandarin oranges, cut in half

METHOD:

1. Heat juices.
2. Dissolve gelatin in the hot juice. Add the vinegar.
3. Allow to cool until the consistency of whipped cream.
4. Fold the other ingredients into the gelatin.
5. Pour into a well-greased 8 x 8 inch pan. Refrigerate until congealed.
6. Cut into squares and serve on a leaf of lettuce. Top each salad with a serving of Whipped Cream Dressing.

Yields 12 servings.

BAYOU SALAD

1⅓ tablespoons plain gelatin
⅔ cup beef broth, cold
(could use bouillon
cubes)
2 cups tomato juice, hot
¼ cup olive juice
⅓ teaspoon salt
⅛ teaspoon pepper
1 cup fine-cut celery
1 cup chopped stuffed olives
1 cup drained cut canned
okra

METHOD:

1. Sprinkle the gelatin over the cold beef broth. Allow to stand 5 minutes.
2. Dissolve gelatin in the hot tomato juice. Add the salt, pepper, and olive juice.
3. Allow to cool until the consistency of whipped cream.
4. Fold in the celery, olives, and okra.
5. Place in a well-oiled 8 x 8 inch pan and refrigerate until congealed.
6. Cut into squares and serve each on a lettuce leaf.
7. Top salad with Whipped Cream Dressing.

Yields 12 servings.

CARMINE SALAD

1 package, pint size, cherry gelatin dessert powder
¾ cup sour red cherry juice, heated (No. 303 can yields ¾ cup juice)
½ cup sugar
¾ cup orange juice
¼ cup vinegar
1 teaspoon almond extract
1 cup cubed canned beets
1 cup red sour cherries, cut in half
1 cup celery, cut in small diced pieces

METHOD:

1. Dissolve the gelatin in the cherry juice. Add the sugar. Add orange juice, vinegar, and extract. Mix.
2. Place the mixture in the refrigerator until slightly thickened.
3. Add the beets, cherries, and celery. Stir together.
4. Place salad in a well-oiled, use salad oil, 8 x 8 inch pan. Return the salad to the refrigerator until it has congealed.
5. Serve with Whipped Cream Dressing on each cut square of salad, which has been placed on a lettuce leaf.

Serves 12.

COCONUT SLAW FOR RELISH TRAYS

2 cups chopped cabbage
¾ cup sugar
½ cup chopped green pepper
1 cup coconut
½ cup vinegar

METHOD:

1. Blend ingredients together.
2. Chill.

Serves 12.

FROSTY FRUIT SALAD

1 egg yolk, beaten
½ cup pineapple juice
1 tablespoon cornstarch
¾ cup mayonnaise
1½ cups whipped cream
2 sliced bananas
3 cups mixed fruit cocktail,
   drained, 1 pound 14 oz.
   can, size No. 2½
¼ cup maraschino cherries,
   cut up

METHOD:

1. Beat egg, add pineapple juice and cornstarch. Stir to mix smooth.

2. Place in the top of a double boiler and cook until thickened. Cool mixture.
3. Fold in the mayonnaise. Next fold in the whipped cream.
4. Fold in the fruit.
5. Place in a well-oiled, use salad oil, 8 x 8 inch pan.
6. Place in the freezer overnight.
7. Cut into squares and serve each cut on a piece of lettuce. Serve with a dopple of whipped cream dressing.

Whipped cream dressing is made with equal parts of whipped cream and mayonnaise mixed together.

Serves 12.

HOLLY BERRY SALAD

1 pint thick applesauce
¼ cup cinnamon imperials (red hots)
2 cups water
1 package Strawberry Jello
1 cup finely chopped celery
¼ cup coarsely chopped walnuts
½ cup whipped cream
½ cup mayonnaise
drop of green coloring
¼ teaspoon cinnamon

METHOD:

1. Boil cinnamon imperials in water until candy is dissolved.
2. Add Jello. Stir to dissolve.
3. Cool. When slightly thickened add applesauce, celery, and walnuts.
4. Pour into a well oiled 8 x 8 inch pan. Refrigerate until congealed.
5. Top each serving with dressing made of whipped cream, mayonnaise, cinnamon, and green coloring.

Serves 10.

JELLIED CITRUS SALAD

2 cups grapefruit juice
1 package lemon gelatin
dessert powder
2 cups cottage cheese
½ cup chopped green pepper
½ cup fine-cut celery

METHOD:

1. Heat the juice and dissolve the gelatin in it.
2. Cool until mixture is consistency of whipped cream. Beat with an electric beater until light and fluffy.
3. Fold the cheese, peppers, and celery into the mixture.
4. Pour into a well-oiled 8 x 8 inch pan. Refrigerate until congealed.
5. Cut into squares and serve each on a leaf of lettuce. Top with Whipped Cream Dressing.

Yields 12 servings.

JONATHAN SALAD

1 cup apples, cut into small cubes
1 cup cut fine celery
¼ cup raisins
¼ cup chopped pecans
½ cup mayonnaise
½ cup whipped cream
¼ cup sour cream
2 teaspoons sugar
1 teaspoon cinnamon

METHOD:

1. Combine and mix together the first 7 ingredients.
2. Place salad in lettuce cups or in one large salad bowl. Sprinkle the cinnamon sugar over the top of the salad.

Serves 8 to 10.

KIDNEY BEAN RELISH

1 tablespoon cornstarch
¼ cup water
¾ cup vinegar
⅛ teaspoon dry mustard
½ teaspoon salt
¼ teaspoon pepper
8 tablespoons sugar

2 cups canned kidney beans.
Rinse in cold water and
drain, size No. 303 can
1 cup fine-cut cabbage
1 cup fine-cut celery
½ cup fine-chopped onion

METHOD:

1. Combine the first 7 ingredients and cook for 5 minutes.
2. Add the other ingredients and mix together.
3. Chill in refrigerator several hours before serving.

Yields 3½ cups of relish.

MALAGA SALAD

1 cup red grapes, cut in half,
seeds removed
2 cups lettuce, torn into
small pieces
3 tablespoons salad oil
1 tablespoon wine vinegar
¼ teaspoon crushed rose-
mary leaves

METHOD:

1. Mix all together and allow to marinate for ½ hour before serving.

Serves 4.

MEXICALI SALAD

  1 package lemon Jello
1½ cups hot water
  ¼ cup vinegar
  1 cup drained and rinsed kidney beans
  1 cup finely chopped cabbage
  ¼ cup chopped green pepper
  1 cup fresh cooked green peas
  ¼ cup lemon juice

METHOD:

1. Dissolve Jello in hot water; add vinegar.
2. Add remaining ingredients to cooled, slightly thickened Jello.
3. Place in oiled pan to set. Use 8 x 8 inch pan.

Serves 8 to 10.

ORIENTAL SALAD

  2 tablespoons plain gelatin
  ½ cup cold water
  3 cups chicken broth, remove the fat (you could

use bouillon cubes—2
cubes per cup of water)
6 tablespoons lemon juice
6 tablespoons Soy Sauce
1 cup diced celery
2 cups drained bean sprouts,
chop with a knife to cut
sprouts in two
½ cup chopped dill pickle
½ cup fine-cut green pepper
¼ cup fine-cut green onion

METHOD:

1. Sprinkle the gelatin over the cold water and allow mixture to stand 5 minutes.
2. Heat the broth and dissolve the gelatin in the hot liquid.
3. Add the lemon juice and Soy Sauce. Mix together.
4. Place the mixture in the refrigerator to chill until the consistency of whipped cream.
5. Add the remaining ingredients and mix together.
6. Grease an 8 x 8 inch cake pan with salad oil and pour the gelatin mixture into the pan. Refrigerate until congealed.
7. Cut salad into squares and serve each cut on a piece of lettuce. Serve with a dash of Whipped Cream Dressing.

Yields 12 to 16 cuts of salad.

ROYAL PURPLE SALAD

1 box of cherry gelatin dessert powder, enough for 1 pint
1 No. 300 can of blueberries, 15 ounce can
½ cup drained pickled watermelon rind, cut up
1 cup orange juice
1 tablespoon lemon juice
1 cup whipped cream mixed with 1 cup mayonnaise

METHOD:

1. Drain the blueberries. Measure the juice and add watermelon pickle juice to make one cup.
2. Heat the above juice with the orange juice. Add the gelatin powder and stir to dissolve. Place in the refrigerator to chill until slightly thickened.
3. Add the blueberries and watermelon pickle.
4. Grease an 8 x 8 inch pan with salad oil. Place the gelatin mixture in the pan and refrigerate until congealed.
5. Cut into servings and place on a lettuce leaf.
6. Serve with a tablespoon of the whipped cream dressing over the top of the salad.

Serves 12.

SEASONABLE SALAD

1 package orange gelatin dessert powder
1 package cherry gelatin dessert powder
1 cup tart apples, cut in small cubes
1 cup cabbage, shredded or chopped fine
½ cup raisins
1 cup carrots, shredded and chopped fine
1 cup crushed pineapple, drained
1 cup pineapple juice
¼ cup vinegar
2¾ cups boiling water

METHOD:

1. Dissolve the gelatin in the boiling water.
2. Add the vinegar and pineapple juice.
3. Place gelatin mixture in the refrigerator to cool and become thickened to the consistency of whipped cream.
4. Add all other ingredients.
5. Place the salad in an oiled 8 x 8 inch pan. Refrigerate until congealed.
6. Cut into squares and serve on a lettuce leaf, top with Whipped Cream Dressing.

Yields 12 servings.

SNOWFLAKE SALAD

3 ounces lemon gelatin dessert powder, 1 package
1¾ cups frozen lemonade (made up)
1 cup minute type rice
1 teaspoon salt
2 tablespoons oleomargarine
1¼ cups water
½ cup whipped cream
½ cup mayonnaise
1 cup diced canned pears
1 cup diced bananas
whipped cream dressing

METHOD:

1. Heat the lemonade to the boiling point and dissolve the gelatin. Cool until at thickening stage.
2. Cook the rice with the salt, water, and oleomargarine until tender. Package gives directions for cooking.
3. When gelatin is thick as whipped cream add the rice which has been drained of any moisture. Whip with an electric beater until light and fluffy.
4. Fold in the fruit. Place the salad in an oiled pan to refrigerate. Use 8 x 8 inch pan.
5. When congealed, cut in squares and serve with Whipped Cream Dressing.

Yields 8 dinner salads.

WHIPPED CREAM DRESSING is made by combining whipped cream and mayonnaise, half and half.

TANGIERS SALAD

1 package orange gelatin dessert powder

1¼ cups orange juice

¼ cup juice from pickled fruit, from p i c k l e d peaches or watermelon

½ cup juice from canned peaches

1 tablespoon vinegar, cider vinegar 5% acidity

½ stick of cinnamon

3 whole cloves

1½ cups carrots, chopped very fine, shred raw, then chop

½ cup fine-cut celery

1 cup sliced peaches, cut up

red food coloring, to give an orange red color

METHOD:

1. Mix the orange juice, pickled fruit juice, peach juice, vinegar, stick cinnamon and cloves together and boil for 5 minutes. Remove the cinnamon and cloves.
2. Dissolve the gelatin in the hot liquid. Add the coloring.
3. Chill mixture until it is the consistency of whipped cream.

4. Add the remaining ingredients and place in a well-oiled 8 x 8 inch pan. Refrigerate until congealed.
5. Cut in squares and serve on a lettuce leaf. Top with Whipped Cream Dressing.

Yields 9 servings.

THREE TONE SALAD PLATE

Place lettuce leaves forming three cups on a large plate. In the center of each leaf place a serving of each of the three following salads. Garnish your plate with sections of hard-cooked eggs, quarters of tomatoes, and black olives.

Potato Salad

Use your favorite potato salad recipe

Chicken Salad

1 cup cubed cooked chicken
½ cup cut pecans
¼ cup fine-cut celery
½ cup cream dressing
(make by mixing half whipped cream with half mayonnaise)
2 teaspoons lemon juice
salt and pepper to taste

METHOD:

1. Combine all ingredients together.

Ham Salad

½ cup cut fine green pepper
ham
1 cup small cubed cooked
½ cup cut slices of black olives
¼ teaspoon chopped chives
2 teaspoons lemon juice
½ cup mayonnaise
salt and pepper to taste

METHOD:

1. Combine all ingredients together.

Yields 4 Salad Plates for Luncheon or Supper Meal.

WHIPPED CREAM DRESSING

1 cup whipped cream
½ cup mayonnaise

METHOD:

1. Fold the mayonnaise into the whipped cream.
2. Serve with jellied salads.

Yields 6-8 servings.

This simple salad dressing is best with jellied salads.

NOTES

NOTES

NOTES

Breads
and
Rolls

APPLE SAUCE BREAD

¼ cup butter
½ cup sugar
2 well-beaten eggs
2 cups flour (sift before measuring)
2 teaspoons baking powder
1 teaspoon salt
⅛ teaspoon baking soda
1 cup thick apple sauce
½ cup buttermilk
2 tablespoons sugar mixed with 1 teaspoon cinnamon

METHOD:

1. Cream the butter and sugar well.
2. Add eggs, mix well. Add apple sauce, mix.
3. Sift the flour, baking powder and salt.
4. Mix the soda with the buttermilk.
5. Add the flour mixture alternately with the buttermilk, beginning and ending with some of the flour.
6. Mix well. Place in a well-greased 9 x 5½ inch loaf pan.
7. Sprinkle the cinnamon sugar over the top of the bread.
8. Bake at 350 F. for 50 minutes. Remove bread from the oven and turn out of pan on its side to cool on a rack or a towel.

Yields one loaf of bread.

BLACK FOREST COFFEE CAKE

1 cup sugar
½ cup butter
2 beaten eggs
2 cups flour (sift before measuring)
1 teaspoon salt
4 teaspoons baking powder
1 cup milk
2 tart apples, peeled and sliced into thin section pieces
½ cup brown sugar
⅛ teaspoon nutmeg
⅛ teaspoon cloves
confectioners' sugar

METHOD:

1. Cream sugar and butter.
2. Sift flour, salt, and baking powder.
3. Add beaten eggs to creamed mixture.
4. Add the flour mixture to the creamed mixture alternately with the milk. Begin and end with some of the flour mixture.
5. Mix well and place in a well greased 9 x 13 inch cake pan. Batter should be ¼ inch thick.
6. Place the apple slices in rows across the top of the batter. Press apples in slightly to hold them in place.
7. Mix the brown sugar with the nutmeg and cloves. Sprinkle this sugar mixture over the apples.

8. Bake at 375 F. for 20 minutes.
9. Remove from oven and cool. Next sift confectioners' sugar over the top of the cake.

Yields 20 to 24 square cuts.

BLACK WALNUT HONEY MUFFINS

½ cup honey
½ cup butter
2 eggs
1 cup sifted whole wheat flour
1 cup sifted white flour
3 teaspoons baking powder
¼ teaspoon salt
1½ cups milk
½ cup chopped black walnuts

METHOD:

1. Blend honey and butter.
2. Add eggs, beat until smooth.
3. Sift together flour, baking powder, and salt.
4. Add alternately with milk, beginning and ending with some of the flour mixture.
5. Fold in the nuts.
6. Place 1 tablespoon in each cup of a small muffin tin, well greased.
7. Bake at 400 F. for 12-15 minutes.

Yields 4 dozen small muffins.

BRAN BREAD

2 cups all bran
1 cup flour
1 cup sour cream
1 cup milk
¾ teaspoon soda
½ cup sugar
1 teaspoon baking powder
2 eggs
1 teaspoon salt
1 cup raisins
½ cup cut pecans

METHOD:

1. Sift flour, salt, sugar and baking powder. Mix nuts and raisins into the flour mixture.
2. Beat eggs well; add the sour cream and soda and mix well.
3. Add the egg mixture to the dry mixture with 1 cup milk.
4. Mix well and bake in well-greased bread pan at 350 F. for 1 hour.
5. Cool for 15 minutes, then turn out onto a rack to cool further.

Yields 1 loaf bread.

CHRISTMAS WREATHS

¼ cup sugar
¾ cup milk
¼ cup butter
1 teaspoon salt
1 package dried yeast dissolved in ¼ cup warm water
2 eggs
4 to 5 cups sifted flour
½ cup butter to cut into the dough later
1 cup diced candied fruit

METHOD:

1. Scald milk, add sugar and salt. When tepid add the dissolved yeast.
2. Add 1 cup of flour and mix. Add the beaten eggs and mix. Add the remaining flour, cup by cup, mixing after each addition. Add only enough flour to make a soft dough.
3. Place dough in a well-greased bowl, grease top of dough and cover with a towel and place in a warm place to let rise until double in bulk.
4. Place dough on a floured board and roll out to ½ inch thickness. Dot the dough over with ¼ cup of the remaining butter.
5. Now fold the dough over as you would a letter for placing in an envelop. With the side of your rolling pin beat

119

the dough to distribute the butter throughout the dough. Roll out again and repeat this process using the remaining ¼ cup of butter.

6. Roll the dough out to ½ inch thickness and cut into strips ¼ inch wide. Shape into circles with a hole in the center as a doughnut. Diameter should be about 3 inches. Place the wreaths on a well-greased baking sheet and allow them to rise double in size.

7. Brush tops with melted butter and sprinkle or arrange candied fruit, cut into small bits, around the rolls as flowers on a wreath.

8. Bake at 375-400 F. for 12 to 15 minutes.

9. Remove from the oven and place rolls on a cookie sheet.

While they are still warm ice with the following icing:

2½ cups confectioners' sugar
4 tablespoons melted butter
4 tablespoons milk

METHOD:

1. Blend sugar and butter. Add the milk and beat until icing is light and creamy.

2. Spread over the tops of the rolls.

Yields 2 dozen rolls.

CRANBERRY BISCUITS

2 cups flour, sift before measuring
1 teaspoon salt
2 tablespoons baking powder
¼ cup lard
¼ teaspoon baking soda
1 cup buttermilk
1 cup chopped fresh or frozen cranberries, measure after chopping
2 tablespoons oleomargarine, melted
granulated sugar to sprinkle tops of biscuits

METHOD:

1. Sift flour, salt, and baking powder.
2. Work the lard into the flour, using finger tips.
3. Mix the soda with the buttermilk and add to the flour mixture.
4. Fold in the cranberries.
5. Roll the dough on a floured pastry board to ½ inch thickness. Cut into rounds, using a small glass for cutting the biscuits. Dip the edge of the glass into some flour before cutting the biscuits to prevent them from sticking to the glass.
6. Place the biscuits on a well-greased cookie sheet, ½ inch apart.

121

7. Brush the tops with the melted oleomargarine and sprinkle generously with the sugar.
8. Bake at 450 F. for 10 to 12 minutes.

Yields 18 biscuits.

CRUMPETS

2 cups sifted flour
1 teaspoon salt
¼ teaspoon baking soda
1½ teaspoons baking powder
⅓ cup lard
1 package dried yeast dissolved in ½ cup warm water
¾ cup buttermilk

METHOD:

1. Sift flour, salt, soda, and baking powder.
2. Work the lard into this mixture as you would for pie crust. Add the buttermilk and yeast mixture. Stir together well.
3. Place dough onto a floured board and roll out to ½ inch thickness. Cut into rounds using a water glass as your cutter or a metal doughnut cutter without the hole. Let rise in a warm place until the rounds are doubled in bulk.
5. Bake at 375 F. on a well-greased cookie sheet for 20

minutes or may cook the crumpet on an electric griddle at 325 F. for 10 to 15 minutes and then turn the crumpet over and cook the other side for 10 minutes.
6. Crumpets are split in half by tearing apart and then toasted. Serve well buttered with jam or honey.

Yields 12 crumpets.

After the Crumpets are cold you tear each apart and toast under the broiler, butter well and serve with jam for breakfast, tea, or as a salad accompaniment.

CRYSTAL GINGER MUFFINS

2 tablespoons butter
3 tablespoons sugar
1 cup sifted flour
¼ teaspoon salt
1½ teaspoons baking powder
¼ teaspoon grated nutmeg
¼ cup milk
¼ cup crystallized ginger, cut fine and mixed in with flour to separate the particles
2 eggs, well beaten

METHOD:

1. Blend butter and sugar.
2. Add eggs and mix well.
3. Sift together flour, salt, baking powder, and nutmeg.
4. Mix in the ginger with the flour mixture.
5. Add flour and milk alternately, beginning and ending with some of the flour.
6. Place about 1 tablespoonful in well-greased small muffin pan cups.
7. Bake at 400 F. for 15-18 minutes.

Yields 20 muffins.

GRANDMOTHER'S BREAD

1 package dried yeast
1⅓ cup tepid water
⅔ cup milk
2 tablespoons lard
2 teaspoons salt
2 teaspoons sugar
5 cups sifted flour
oil

METHOD:

1. Dissolve yeast in water.
2. Heat milk to scald and add lard, salt, and sugar. Stir. Cool until tepid.
3. Add milk mixture to yeast gradually by adding some milk and some flour and mix well after each addition.
4. Grease the top of dough with oil. Grease sides and bottom of a bowl and place dough in it. Cover with a towel and place in warm place to allow to rise double in bulk (about 1½ hours).
5. Place in a well-greased bread pan and allow to rise once more (½ hour).
6. Bake 1 hour at 375 F.
7. Remove from oven, butter top of bread, and turn pan on side to cool.

Yields 1 loaf.

HAZELNUT COFFEE ROLLS

½ cup milk
½ cup sugar
1 tablespoon instant coffee powder
1 teaspoon salt
2 packages dried yeast dissolved in ½ cup warm water
2 well-beaten eggs
3½ cups sifted flour
¼ cup melted oleomargarine
Mix 1 cup shaved hazelnuts with ½ cup of flour

Icing: 6 tablespoons cream
2 tablespoons melted butter
½ teaspoon vanilla extract
2 cups sifted confectioners' sugar

METHOD:

1. Scald the milk and dissolve the sugar, salt, and instant coffee in the hot liquid. Mix well.
2. When the milk has cooled to warm add the dissolved yeast and mix together.
3. Add the melted oleomargarine and mix.
4. Add the eggs and 3½ cups of flour and mix well.
5. Add the hazelnut flour mixture and knead into the

126

dough. This can be accomplished by kneading on a floured board or with your hands kneading in the bowl.

6. Place the dough in a well-greased bowl and also grease the top of the dough. Cover with a cloth and allow the dough to rise and double in bulk, approximately 1 hour and 15 minutes.
7. Punch the dough down and allow to rise again, time 30 minutes.
8. Place the dough on a floured board and roll to ½ inch thickness. Cut into rounds 2½ inch diameter.
9. Place on a well-greased cookie sheet with each circle touching the other. Slash the top of each roll with a very sharp knife, cutting ⅛ inch deep from top to bottom of each circle.
10. Allow the rolls to rise double in bulk, time 30 minutes.
11. Bake at 400 F. for 15 minutes. Cool rolls and ice as follows:
    A. Blend the confectioners' sugar with the butter, cream, and vanilla. Beat until light and creamy.
    B. Spread icing over cooled rolls.

Yields 3 dozen rolls.

These rolls may be heated before serving by placing them in a 150 F. oven, covered, for 10 to 15 minutes. The icing will not then melt.

LEMON BREAD

2 tablespoons butter
½ cup sugar
2 eggs
2 cups sifted flour
2½ teaspoons baking powder
¾ teaspoon salt
½ teaspoon baking soda
grated rind of 2 lemons
½ cup milk
¼ cup lemon juice

METHOD:

1. Cream butter and sugar.
2. Beat eggs and add.
3. Sift together flour, baking powder, soda, and salt.
4. Add lemon rind to flour mixture.
5. Add to creamed mixture alternately with milk. Begin and end with some of the flour.
6. Add lemon juice.
7. Bake in well-greased 9 x 5½ inch loaf pan at 350 F. for 1 hour.
8. Turn out on rack to cool.
9. Frost with the following icing.

ICING FOR LEMON BREAD

1 egg white
½ tablespoon lemon juice
1 cup powdered sugar

METHOD:

1. Beat egg white stiff.
2. Beat in juice and sugar.

LONESOME PINE CORNCAKE

6/76 Ocracoke
2x w/self
rising
+ butter
in 12
sm loaves
20-25
min

2 cups white cornmeal
½ cup sifted flour
½ teaspoon salt
½ cup milk
3 teaspoons baking powder
½ teaspoon baking soda
1½ cups buttermilk
2 well-beaten eggs
5 tablespoons melted lard

METHOD:

1. Sift the flour, cornmeal, baking powder, and salt together.
2. Add the milk to the beaten eggs.
3. Add the egg mixture to the flour mixture and beat well.
4. Mix the baking soda with the buttermilk. Add to the batter and mix well.
5. Add the melted lard and beat well together.
6. Heat a 9 x 13 inch baking pan in a 475 F. oven until it is very hot. Grease the pan well with lard. Pour the batter into the pan and bake at 475 F. for 30 minutes.

Yields 12 to 18 squares.

This cornbread is also good to use in making dressings.

129

MAPLE MUFFINS

3 tablespoons butter
⅓ cup brown sugar, packed
2 eggs
¼ cup maple syrup
1 cup sifted flour (sifted before measuring)
1½ teaspoon baking powder
⅛ teaspoon baking soda
¼ cup buttermilk
¼ teaspoon salt

METHOD:

1. Cream the butter and brown sugar together.
2. Beat the eggs well and beat in the maple syrup.
3. Add to the creamed mixture and blend well.
4. Sift the flour again with baking powder and salt.
5. Mix the baking soda with the buttermilk.
6. Add the flour and buttermilk alternately, beginning and ending with some of the flour.
7. Blend together well.
8. Place batter in well greased muffin tins. Bake at 425 F. for 20 to 25 minutes.

This recipe makes 12 large muffins. You may need to assist the muffin out of each cup as it is a spongy-textured muffin.

ONION ROLLS

1 cake compressed yeast
or packaged dried yeast
¼ cup warm water
¼ cup melted lard
1 cup mashed potatoes
5 cups sifted flour
⅛ cup sugar
2 teaspoons salt
2 beaten eggs
1 cup milk
1 cup finely chopped
onions   * * *

*precoke 7/76
(sticky dough)*

METHOD:

1. Blend yeast and warm water.
2. Add lard and potatoes.
3. Mix flour, sugar, and salt. Add to the above with eggs mixed in milk.
4. Stir in onions.
5. Knead and let rise.
6. Place on floured board and roll to ½ inch thickness. Cut into rounds, 2½ inches diameter. Place on well-greased pan.
7. Let rise.
8. Bake at 400 F. for 15 minutes.

Yields 4-4½ dozen rolls.

PEANUT ROLLS

1 package of dried yeast
dissolved in ¼ cup warm
water
1 cup scalded milk, cool
until tepid
¼ cup melted butter
¼ cup sugar
4½ to 5 cups flour
1 teaspoon salt
2 beaten eggs
1 cup chopped toasted peanuts, without skins

METHOD:

1. Dissolve the yeast in the warm water.
2. Add the butter, sugar, salt, eggs, milk, and 1 cup of flour. Mix well. Add the peanuts and mix well.
3. Add the remaining flour enough to make a soft dough.
4. Place the dough in a well-greased bowl and grease the top of the dough. Cover with a towel and set in a warm place to rise and double in bulk. Time needed about 2 hours.
5. Grease one's hands and pinch off small bits of dough to form a ball the size of a walnut and place 3 pieces in the cup of a well-greased muffin pan. Makes 2 dozen rolls.
6. Let rise until double in bulk. Bake at 375 F. for 15 minutes.

Yields 2 dozen rolls.

PRUNE MUFFINS

½ cup sugar
¼ cup butter
2 cups sifted flour
3 teaspoons baking powder
½ teaspoon salt
½ teaspoon baking soda
1 cup cut-up cooked pitted prunes
2 beaten eggs
¾ cup prune juice

METHOD:

1. Cream sugar and butter.
2. Sift together flour, baking powder, salt, and soda.
3. Add prunes to creamed mixture.
4. Add eggs.
5. Add flour mixture with prune juice.
6. Bake at 400 F. for 15 minutes in small, well-greased, half-filled muffin tins.

Yields 3 dozen small or 2 dozen large muffins.

RAISIN ROLLS

2 packages dried yeast
½ cup warm water
2 cups milk
½ cup oleomargarine
2 well-beaten eggs
6-8 cups sifted flour
¾ cup sugar
1 teaspoon salt
2 cups raisins

METHOD:

1. Dissolve the yeast in the warm water.
2. Scald the milk. Cool until tepid and add the yeast.
3. Measure 4 cups of flour and sift with sugar and salt. Mix the raisins with this.
4. Add this with the eggs to the milk and beat well.
5. Add the remaining flour and mix well. This should be a soft dough. You may not need all the flour.
6. Place in a well-greased bowl and cover with a towel. Set in a warm place to rise double in bulk. About 2 hours.
7. Turn dough out onto a floured board and roll to ½ inch thick. Brush top with melted butter and sprinkle with granulated sugar. Cut into rounds and place on well-greased pan.
8. Let rise until double in size. Bake at 375 F. for 15 minutes.

Yields 5 dozen.

SAFFRON ROLLS

1 cup scalded milk
¼ cup butter
¼ cup sugar
1 teaspoon salt
4½ to 5 cups sifted flour
1 compressed yeast cake or
1 package dried yeast
1 cup finely chopped mixed
candied fruit
½ teaspoon saffron
¼ cup water

METHOD:

1. Add the butter and sugar to the hot milk.
2. If you use dried yeast dissolve the yeast in ¼ cup of warm water, however if you use compressed yeast you may crumble the yeast into the cooled tepid milk and stir to dissolve.
3. Boil the saffron in the ¼ cup water for 1 minute. Strain. Add to the milk mixture.
4. Sift the flour and salt and mix in the fruit bits. This will separate the particles better for mixing.
5. Add the flour. Use 4½ cups and add the other ½ cup if the dough is still too soft. Mix well.
6. Place the dough in a well-greased bowl and grease the top of the dough as well. Cover with a towel and place in a warm place to rise and double in bulk.
7. When dough is ready place three small balls the size

of a walnut in each cup of a well-greased muffin pan. Allow the dough to rise double in size again.

8. Bake in a 375-400 F. oven for 10 to 12 minutes, until rolls are lightly browned.
9. Remove rolls to a tray and frost, while warm, with the following icing.

ICING FOR SAFFRON ROLLS

2 cups confectioners' sugar
2 tablespoons melted butter
4 tablespoons cream
1 teaspoon vanilla

METHOD:

1. Blend sugar and butter.
2. Add other ingredients and beat until light and creamy. Spread on tops of rolls.

Yields 2 to 2½ dozen rolls.

Very festive bread for holiday meals, similar to Welsh Christmas Rolls.

SWEET ROLLS

1 package dried yeast
1 cup milk
4 cups flour
1 teaspoon salt
2 eggs
2 tablespoons sugar
2 tablespoons melted butter

METHOD:

1. Dissolve the yeast in ¼ cup tepid water.
2. Scald milk. Cool until warm and add well-beaten eggs. Add yeast.
3. Measure 2 cups flour and sift with salt and sugar. Add and mix well. Add the melted butter and mix well.
4. Add the other two cups flour to make a soft dough. Mix well.
5. Place in a well-greased bowl, cover and let rise. Place bowl in a warm place. (about 2 hours time needed.)
6. When dough has doubled in bulk, remove to floured pastry board and roll to ½ inch thickness.
7. Prepare following topping:

TOPPING

1 cup brown sugar
1 cup white sugar
2 teaspoons cinnamon
⅛ teaspoon nutmeg
⅛ teaspoon mace
4 tablespoons melted butter
1 cup chopped Brazil nuts
or pecans

METHOD:

1. Mix the two sugars and spices together. Sprinkle over the dough. Distribute the melted butter over the sugar mixture. Next sprinkle the nuts over the top of the dough. Press the nuts down slightly into the dough.
2. Now roll the dough into a roll which makes a tube approximately 2 inches in diameter.
3. Cut slices 2 inches thick from the roll of dough.
4. Dip each slice into melted butter (you will need about ¾ cup for this).
5. Place the rolls in a well-greased pan about ¼ inch apart.
6. Let the rolls rise until they have doubled in size.
7. Bake at 400 F. for 12-15 minutes.

Yields 2½ dozen rolls. They won't last long!

WHOLE WHEAT MUFFINS

½ cup brown sugar
½ cup butter
¼ cup molasses
2 beaten eggs
1 cup flour
1 cup whole wheat flour
2 teaspoons baking powder
¼ teaspoon salt
½ teaspoon baking soda
1¼ cups buttermilk

METHOD:

1. Blend sugar and butter.
2. Add molasses. Blend.
3. Add eggs. Blend.
4. Sift together flour, baking powder, and salt.
5. Mix baking soda into buttermilk.
6. Add flour mixture alternately with the buttermilk. Begin and end with some of the flour.
7. Fill well-greased muffin cups half full.
8. Bake at 400 F. for 12-15 minutes.

Yields 4 dozen small muffins.

NOTES

NOTES

NOTES

Cookies
and
Punches

ALMOND CRISPS

6 tablespoons butter
1 cup sugar
1 beaten egg
2 teaspoons almond extract
1 cup cake flour, sift before measuring
1 teaspoon baking powder
¼ teaspoon salt
½ cup chopped fine almonds

METHOD:

1. Cream butter and sugar.
2. Add egg and mix well.
3. Add extract and beat.
4. Sift flour, baking powder, and salt. Mix the chopped almonds into the flour.
5. Add flour mixture to the creamed mixture and beat well.
6. Chill dough.
7. Form dough into balls the size of a walnut and place on a greased cookie sheet 2 inches apart.
8. Bake 20 minutes at 350 F.

Yields 24 cookies.

ARABIAN KNIGHTS

½ cup butter
½ cup sugar
1 egg well beaten
½ teaspoon mint extract
½ teaspoon vanilla
1 cup flour
1 teaspoon baking powder
2 tablespoons cream

METHOD:

1. Blend sugar and butter.
2. Mix vanilla and mint with beaten egg.
3. Sift flour and baking powder.
4. Put all ingredients together adding the cream. Mix very well.
5. Spread in well-greased 9 x 9 inch baking pan.
6. Sprinkle the following over the top: (sift together) ½ cup sugar, ¼ cup cocoa, ½ teaspoon cinnamon.
7. Bake at 375 F. for 25 minutes.

Yields 36 squares.

BAMBOOZLES

¼ cup oleomargarine
¾ cup sugar
2 well-beaten eggs
1 cup flour, sifted
¼ teaspoon salt
1½ teaspoons cinnamon
½ teaspoon nutmeg
1 teaspoon baking powder
1 cup crushed cornflakes
½ cup currants
½ cup buttermilk
½ teaspoon baking soda

METHOD:

1. Cream the oleomargarine and sugar together. Add eggs and blend.
2. Sift flour with salt, cinnamon, nutmeg, and baking powder.
3. Add cornflakes and currants to the flour mixture.
4. Mix the baking soda with the buttermilk.
5. Add the flour mixture with the buttermilk alternately, beginning and ending with some of the flour mixture, to the creamed mixture.
6. Drop by teaspoonful onto a well-greased cookie sheet.
7. Bake at 375 F. for 10 to 12 minutes.

Yields 76 cookies.

CANTON GINGER COOKIES

1 cup butter
½ cup sugar
½ fine cut crystalized ginger
3 cups sifted flour
4 eggs
½ teaspoon baking soda
1 teaspoon baking powder
½ teaspoon salt

METHOD:

1. Cream the butter and sugar.
2. Beat the egg yolks until light and add the ginger.
3. Mix the eggs with the creamed mixture.
4. Sift the flour, salt, soda, and baking powder.
5. Add to the creamed mixture.
6. Beat the egg whites until light and stiff. Fold these into the cookie mixture.
7. Drop by the teaspoonful onto a well-greased cookie sheet. Place cookies 1 inch apart.
8. Bake at 375 F. for 15 minutes.

Yields 76 cookies.

You may use half the recipe if you desire fewer cookies.

CHEESE NOTHINGNESS

1 cup boiling water
½ cup grated sharp yellow cheese
1 cup sifted flour
4 eggs

METHOD:

1. Bring water to a rolling boil.
2. Add cheese and stir to dissolve.
3. Add flour and cook, stirring until it forms a ball.
4. Cool mixture until warm and add the eggs one at a time, beating well after each addition.
5. Drop from tip of spoon into small muffin pans, filling each cup just over half full.
6. Bake at 375 F. for 20 minutes.

Yields 3 dozen tidbits.

COCONUT MACAROONS

1 egg white
1 cup confectioners' sugar
1 cup fine-cut coconut
½ teaspoon vanilla extract

METHOD:

1. Beat egg white until frothy and standing in peaks.
2. Fold in the sugar and coconut.
3. Drop by teaspoonful onto a well-greased cookie sheet.
4. Bake at 325 F. for 15 to 20 minutes.
5. Remove from the oven and allow to set 10 minutes. Lift from the pan using a spatula.

Yields 20 macaroons.

A VERY NICE DESSERT MAY ALSO BE MADE BY CRUMBLING THE MACAROONS AND ROLLING AN ICE CREAM BALL IN THEM. TOP WITH FUDGE SAUCE.

DATE FRIVOLITIES

2 cups cake flour, sift before
measuring
½ teaspoon salt
1 cup sugar
1 cup oleomargarine
½ cup buttermilk
1 teaspoon baking soda
2 cups uncooked oatmeal
1 pound dates, cut up
2 well-beaten eggs
confectioners' sugar

METHOD:

1. Sift the flour and salt together.
2. Blend the sugar and oleomargarine.
3. Mix the soda with the buttermilk.
4. Add 1 cup of flour and 2 cups of oatmeal with the buttermilk. Mix well.
5. Add the beaten eggs and mix well.
6. Mix the other cup of flour with the dates, to separate the particles.
7. Add the flour and dates and mix well.
8. Drop by teaspoonful onto a well-greased cookie sheet.
9. Bake at 375 F. for 15 minutes. Toss cookies in the confectioners' sugar to coat them well.

Yields 100 cookies. You could easily cut the recipe in half if fewer cookies are desired.

DESERT BARS

½ cup sugar
⅓ cup butter
½ cup flour, sift before measuring

METHOD:

1. Cream butter and sugar. Next work in the flour with a fork or fingertips. Shape into a ball and place in the center of an 8 inch square pan.
2. Spread this mixture out over the bottom of the pan with your fingers.
3. Bake at 350 F. for 10 minutes.

WHILE THIS MIXTURE IS BAKING PREPARE THE FOLLOWING:

⅓ cup honey
1 egg, well beaten
½ cup flour
½ teaspoon baking powder
⅛ teaspoon salt
½ cup chopped brazil nuts
½ cup chopped dates
½ cup sesame seeds

PROCEDURE:

A. Mix the honey and egg together.
B. Sift the flour with the salt and baking powder.
C. Mix the nuts, dates, and seeds with the flour.

D. Add the flour mixture to the egg mixture.
E. Spread over the now baked first mixture right after you remove it from the oven.
F. Bake at 350 F. for 20 minutes.
G. Cool and cut into small bars.

Yields 24 two inch bars.

FANDANGOS

¼ cup butter
¾ cup brown sugar
2 beaten egg yolks
¾ cup flour
1 cup cut fine marshmallows
½ cup coconut
½ cup candied fruit, cut fine
½ cup chopped pecans
2 stiffly beaten egg whites

METHOD:

1. Cream butter and brown sugar.
2. Add egg yolks. Blend.
3. Add flour and rub together to mix well.
4. Pat mixture in bottom of a well-greased 9 x 13 inch pan.
5. Bake at 350 F. for 10 minutes.
6. Mix marshmallow, coconut, fruit, pecans and combine with the egg whites.
7. Spread on top of the baked crust and return to the oven for 20 minutes.
8. Cut into 2 x 2 inch squares.

Yields 24 cookies.

GINGERBREAD MEN

½ cup New Orleans molasses
½ teaspoon salt
½ cup butter
1 cup sugar
3 well-beaten eggs
5 cups sifted flour
½ teaspoon baking soda mixed with 2 tablespoons buttermilk
½ tablespoon powdered ginger

METHOD:

1. Cream the butter and sugar.
2. Add the eggs, mix well, add the molasses and mix well.
3. Sift the flour, ginger, and salt.
4. Add the flour with the buttermilk to the egg mixture.
5. Blend well. Place on floured board and roll out very thin.
6. Cut with a gingerbread man cutter or other cookie shapes. Place these on a well-greased cookie sheet pan.
7. Sprinkle the tops with a mixture of:
   1 tablespoon powdered ginger and ½ cup sugar.
8. Bake 6 to 10 minutes until well browned, but not burned, at 450 F.

Yields 94 round cookies 2½ inch diameter or about 3 dozen gingerbread men, depending on the size of your cookie cutter.

154

HEALTHY, WEALTHY, AND WISE COOKIES

⅔ cup brown sugar
½ cup butter
1 beaten egg
1 cup sifted cake flour
½ cup all bran
½ cup raisins
¼ cup buttermilk
¼ teaspoon baking soda

METHOD:

1. Cream butter and sugar.
2. Add the egg and mix well.
3. Mix the flour, raisins, and all bran together.
4. Mix the soda with the buttermilk.
5. Add the flour mixture alternately with the buttermilk. Begin and end with some of the flour mixture.
6. Drop by teaspoonful, about the size of a walnut, onto a well-greased cookie sheet.
7. Bake at 375 F. for 12 minutes or until browned.

Yields 4½ dozen cookies.

NEW AMSTERDAMS

½ cup butter
1 cup confectioners' sugar
1 cup flour (sift before measuring)
½ cup Dutch process cocoa
½ cup chopped nuts
1 teaspoon vanilla
2 tablespoons cream

METHOD:

1. Blend sugar and butter.
2. Sift flour and cocoa together.
3. Add flour mixture, nuts, cream, and vanilla to the creamed mixture. Blend together.
4. Shape the dough into small balls about the size of a walnut.
5. Bake on a well-greased cookie sheet for 20 minutes at 300 F.

Yields 40 cookies.

PEANUT BUTTER FOLLYS

½ cup butter
4 eggs
2 cups sugar
½ teaspoon salt
1 teaspoon vanilla
1½ cups flour, sift before measuring
¾ cup peanut butter

METHOD:

1. Cream butter, peanut butter, and sugar.
2. Beat the eggs well and add. Add the salt and vanilla. Mix well.
3. Add the flour and blend together.
4. Bake in a well-greased 9 x 13 inch pan at 350 F. for 40 minutes.
5. Cut into squares while warm.

Yields 32 cookies.

TARPAN COOKIES

3 eggs, beaten until light
¾ cup sugar
1 cup pastry flour, sift before measuring
½ teaspoon cream of tartar
½ teaspoon baking soda
1 teaspoon lemon extract

METHOD:

1. Add the sugar to the eggs. Whip until creamy.
2. Sift flour, soda, and cream of tartar.
3. Add flour mixture and extract to the egg mixture and blend.
4. Drop by teaspoonfuls onto a well-greased cookie sheet.
5. Bake at 375-400 F. for 10 minutes until lightly browned.

Yields 70 cookies.

CARNELIAN PUNCH

2 cups prune juice
2 cups apple juice
2 cups grapefruit juice
red coloring

METHOD:

Mix juices together. Add enough red coloring to give a carnelian color.

Yields 8-10 servings.

CIDER PUNCH CUP

3 cups apple cider
1 cup grapejuice
1 cup orange juice, fresh or frozen
¼ cup lemon juice

METHOD:

1. Mix all ingredients together.
2. Chill and serve.

Yields 8-10 servings.

GARNET PUNCH

2½ cups cranberry juice
2½ cups grape juice

METHOD:

Mix the 2 juices. Chill and serve.

Yields 8-10 servings.

Bottled cranberry juice is used. If you prefer fresh, cook the berries and water until the berries pop open, then press mixture through a sieve. Sweeten to taste.

RHUBARB NECTAR PUNCH

1 one pound package frozen rhubarb
1 quart water
½ cup sugar
¼ cup lemon juice, about 2 lemons

METHOD:

1. Cook the rhubarb, sugar, and water for 10 minutes.
2. Strain and chill. Add the lemon juice. Mix.

Yields 8 servings.

If fresh rhubarb is used you will need to cook until soft. You will also need to increase the amount of sugar for sweetening.

TOMATO JUICE SUPREME

2 cups tomato juice
2 tablespoons lemon juice
½ teaspoon pepper
¼ teaspoon salt
⅛ teaspoon celery salt
⅛ teaspoon thyme
⅛ teaspoon onion salt

METHOD:

1. Mix all ingredients together and chill well.
2. Mix again before serving.

Yields 4 servings.

NOTES

NOTES

NOTES

Desserts

BOONE TAVERN CHERRY SAUCE

1 one pound can of sour red
     cherries, can Number 303
2½ cups sugar

METHOD:

1. Mix the cherries and juice with the sugar. Cook at a rolling boil until your candy thermometer reaches 220 F. or about 10 minutes of cooking time.
2. Cool the sauce.
3. Serve over ice cream or as a pudding sauce.

Yields 16 servings.

BUTTERED HAZELNUT SUNDAE

2 cups brown sugar
⅛ pound butter
2 cups cream
1 cup (cut fine) hazelnuts

METHOD:

1. Place the sugar in a heavy skillet or pan and melt sugar. Stir during this process, about 10 minutes. Do not burn.
2. Add the butter and mix. This will not mix well but now add the cream slowly and stir to prevent lumping.
3. Add the nuts and mix well.
4. Cool and serve over ice cream.

Serves 8-10.

CAPRICE PUDDING

½ cup oleomargarine
1 cup brown sugar
1 beaten egg
1 teaspoon almond extract
1½ cups pastry flour, sift before measuring
1 teaspoon baking powder
½ cup milk
1 cup marshmallows, cut fine
½ cup chopped pecans
1 cup canned apricots, cut
in pieces (drain well)

METHOD:

1. Cream the oleomargarine and sugar well.
2. Add the egg and extract. Mix well.
3. Sift the flour and baking powder.
4. Add flour with the milk to the egg mixture.
5. Spread this mixture in a 9 x 13 inch well-greased pan.
6. Mix the pecans, apricots, and marshmallows. Spread over the batter.
7. Bake at 400 F. for 20 to 30 minutes.
8. Cut into squares and serve warm with whipped cream.

Yields 20 servings.

CHOCOLATE FUDGE SAUCE

1 cup brown sugar
1 cup white sugar
⅛ teaspoon salt
⅔ cup cocoa (Dutch process cocoa)
2 tablespoons cornstarch
2 cups coffee cream
3 tablespoons butter
1 teaspoon vanilla extract

METHOD:

1. Sift the sugars, salt, cocoa, and cornstarch together.
2. Add the cream and blend well.
3. Cook until a temperature of 215 F. on your candy thermometer is reached or until the mixture is just before the soft ball stage when tested by dropping a bit into a small amount of cold water.
4. Remove from the fire and add the vanilla and butter, blend.
5. Cool and then refrigerate so that the sauce may thicken.

Yields 3 cups of sauce or 24 one-ounce servings.

For a hot fudge sauce I would suggest using 3½ tablespoons of cornstarch for thickening.

CHOCOLATE TRUFFLE SUNDAE

1 tablespoon flour
½ cup sugar
¼ teaspoon salt
2½ tablespoons cocoa
1 cup milk
2 egg yolks
4 tablespoons butter
½ teaspoon vanilla
6 ounces plum jam or plum butter
1 cup finely cut dates

METHOD:

1. Sift flour with the sugar, salt, and cocoa.
2. Add milk. Stir until smooth.
3. Place in the top of a double boiler and cook for 12 minutes. Stir to prevent lumping.
4. Beat egg yolks well. Add to the above mixture and cook for 3 minutes. Stir often. A wire whip is helpful in the stirring process.
5. Remove from the heat. Add the butter, vanilla, jam, and dates.
6. Cool mixture.
7. Serve over ice cream or you may like to use this sauce over a pudding.

Serves 10 to 12.

DEVIL'S DELIGHT

½ cup butter
1 cup sugar
2 eggs, well beaten
1 cup sifted cake flour
¼ teaspoon salt
¾ teaspoon baking soda
⅓ cup buttermilk
1½ squares bitter chocolate
⅓ cup cooked coffee
½ teaspoon vanilla

METHOD:

1. Cream butter and sugar.
2. Add eggs. Mix.
3. Sift flour and salt together.
4. Mix baking soda with the buttermilk.
5. Add the flour mixture and buttermilk alternately to the creamed mixture, beginning and ending with some of the flour. Mix well.
6. Stir chocolate into boiling coffee. Stir until smooth.
7. Add to cake batter while coffee mixture is hot. Mix well.
8. Add vanilla. Beat well.
9. Bake in a well greased 9 x 13 inch pan for 45 minutes at 325 F.
10. Cool and cover with the filling topping which you may prepare while the cake part is baking:

TOPPING FOR DEVIL'S DELIGHT

¼ cup cold water
1 tablespoon gelatin (plain)
pinch of salt
¼ cup cold water
2 cups milk
1 cup sugar
½ cup Dutch process cocoa
1 pint whipping cream,
whipped
¼ cup grated sweet chocolate
1 teaspoon vanilla

METHOD:

1. Sprinkle the gelatin over the cold water.
2. Place the milk in the top of a double boiler and heat.
3. Sift the sugar with the cocoa. Add to the hot milk and stir to dissolve. Add salt.
4. Add the gelatin and stir to dissolve.
5. Place the filling to cool and when it begins to thicken fold in the whipped cream and vanilla.
6. Spread filling over the cooled cake and top with a sprinkling of the grated chocolate.
7. Refrigerate until serving time. This takes 3 to 4 hours.
8. Cut into 20 squares and top each with a dash of whipped cream.

Serves 20 for a dessert or less if dessert and beverage are all you are serving.

DROMEDARY SUNDAE SAUCE

1 cup dates, finely cut
⅔ cup sugar
¾ cup water
½ teaspoon almond extract

METHOD:

1. Combine dates, sugar, and water. Cook slowly to thicken mixture, approximately 10 minutes.
2. Remove from the fire and add the extract.
3. Cool and serve over ice cream or as a pudding sauce.

Serves 8.

DUBARRY SUNDAE SAUCE

1 cup sugar
½ cup milk
2 tablespoons butter
½ teaspoon wintergreen flavoring
¼ teaspoon mint extract
green food coloring

173

METHOD:

1. Cook sugar and milk to 200 F.
2. Add butter and flavorings.
3. Color green.

Serves 8.

ENGLISH TRIFLE

1 dozen lady fingers
(can be purchased at
bakery shop)
2 cups milk
½ package lemon gelatin
dessert powder
3 tablespoons cornstarch
2 egg yolks, well beaten
2 egg whites, stiffly beaten
½ cup sugar
1 cup vanilla cookies, rolled
fine
¾ cup orange juice
¼ cup maraschino cherries,
chopped
½ cup chopped almonds
3 cups whipped cream
½ cup grated coconut

METHOD:

1. Pour the orange juice over the crushed vanilla cookies. Allow to stand 5 minutes.
2. Mix the sugar with the cornstarch. Add the milk and stir to produce a smooth mixture.
3. Cook the milk mixture in the top of a double boiler for 10 minutes until it begins to thicken. Add the egg yolks and cook 3 minutes.
4. Remove from the heat and add the gelatin and stir to dissolve.
5. Add the stiffly beaten egg whites.
6. Cool the mixture and add the cookies, cherries, and almonds. Fold in the whipped cream.
7. Line a ring mold (a spring mold in which the sides can be removed) with the lady fingers. You split the lady fingers in half and then cut each in two. Lay the fingers around the bottom of the tin and stand them around the sides.
8. Pour in the mixture and refrigerate several hours.
9. Remove the outer ring and place the pudding on a serving plate by lifting off the bottom pan with help of a pancake turner.
10. Garnish the top with additional sweetened whipped cream and sprinkle the coconut over the top.

Serves 20. Perhaps fewer as most will wish a generous helping.

FLORENTINE COFFEE SAUCE

1 tablespoon cornstarch
½ cup whipping cream
1 pint coffee cream
½ cup sugar
1 tablespoon instant coffee powder
2 teaspoons brandy extract

METHOD:

1. Mix the cornstarch with the ½ cup of cream.
2. Add the sugar and the pint of cream.
3. Cook in top of a double boiler until thickened.
4. Add the instant coffee powder and blend.
5. Add the extract and blend.
6. Cool and serve over ice cream or pudding as a sauce.

Serves 12.

FRESH PINEAPPLE MINT SUNDAE

2 teaspoons finely chopped fresh mint
1⅓ cups crushed pineapple
1 cup sugar
⅓ cup pineapple juice

METHOD:

1. Mix ingredients. Cook 15 minutes to 200 F.
2. Serve over ice cream.

You may use dried mint leaves if fresh not available.

Serves 12.

FRESH RASPBERRY SUNDAE, VIENNE

20 ounces frozen red raspberries
1 cup sugar
¼ cup water

METHOD:

1. Mix 10 ounces of the raspberries with the sugar and water.
2. Boil for 10 minutes.
3. Cool and add 10 ounces of raspberries.
4. Serve over ice cream or use for parfait sauce.

Serves 8-10.

KENTUCKY BLACKBERRY DUMPLING WITH MILK DIP

Prepare pie crust, recipe page 230
- 1 can blackberries, 15 ounce size
- 2 tablespoons cornstarch
- ½ cup sugar
- pinch of salt
- liquid from blackberries
- 1 tablespoon butter
- 1 teaspoon lemon juice

METHOD:

1. Roll out pie crust and cut each circle into 4 pie-shape wedges. Crust should make 2 circles.
2. Drain the blackberries.
3. Place the blackberry juice mixed with the cornstarch, sugar, and salt in the top of a double boiler and cook to thicken. Remove from the heat and add the butter, lemon juice, and berries.
4. Place a good tablespoon of berry mixture in the center of each pie crust wedge and bring edges together, pinching to close the dumpling.
5. Bake the dumplings at 450 F. for 15 minutes.
6. Serve each warm with the warm Milk Dip.

DIP RECIPE:

> 3 cups milk
> ¾ cup sugar
> 2½ tablespoons cornstarch
> 6 tablespoons butter
> 1½ teaspoons vanilla

METHOD:

A. Mix the sugar and cornstarch.
B. Heat the milk in the top of a double boiler.
C. Add the sugar mixture and cook until thickened, stir to prevent lumping.
D. Add the butter and vanilla.

Serve each dumpling with a generous amount of Dip.

Yields 8 dumplings.

NORWEGIAN CREAM CAKE

1½ cups sugar
1 cup cake flour, sift before measuring
½ teaspoon salt
1 teaspoon cream of tartar
1 teaspoon baking powder
12 egg whites
1 teaspoon vanilla extract
4 cups sweetened whipped cream
3 16-ounce packages frozen strawberries

METHOD:

1. Sift flour, salt, cream of tartar, and baking powder 4 times.
2. Beat the egg whites until stiff and light. Add the sugar to the egg whites.
3. Fold in the flour mixture using light sweeping strokes to incorporate as much air as possible.
4. Fold in the vanilla.
5. Bake in an ungreased angel food cake tin. Use a 10 inch pan. If you use a smaller cake tin reduce the egg whites to 9. Bake at 325 F. for 1 hour.
6. Turn cake face down on a towel to cool. Next split cake into three layers with a sharp knife.
7. Fill each layer with a spread of the whipped cream and a portion of the strawberries. Top the cake and

sides with whipped cream and strawberries on top Allow some of the juice to dribble down over the sides. Refrigerate before serving.

Yields 20 servings.

THIS ALSO MAKES A FINE-GRAINED ANGEL FOOD CAKE FOR OTHER USES.

OLD FASHIONED CHOCOLATE PUDDING WITH EGG SAUCE

4 tablespoons flour
1 cup sugar
⅛ teaspoon salt
5 tablespoons cocoa
   (Dutch process type)
2 cups milk
3 egg yolks, well beaten
9 tablespoons oleomargarine
1 teaspoon vanilla

TOPPING EGG SAUCE

4 egg yolks, well beaten
½ cup sugar
¼ teaspoon salt
1 tablespoon cornstarch
2 cups cold milk
2 teaspoons vanilla

METHODS:

For Pudding

1. Sift the flour, sugar, salt, and cocoa.
2. Add the milk and stir until smooth.
3. Place in the top of a double boiler and cook for 12 minutes, stirring to prevent lumping.
4. Add egg yolks, stir and cook for 3 minutes.
5. Remove from the heat and add the oleomargarine and vanilla.
6. Pour into sherbet cups. Fills 10 to 12 cups.

For Egg Sauce

A. Add sugar and salt to the beaten egg yolks.
B. Blend the milk with the cornstarch to form a smooth mixture.
C. Cook this mixture in the top of a double boiler until slightly thickened, stir to prevent lumping.
D. Remove from the heat and add the vanilla.
E. Cool sauce and serve over the pudding.

Yields 10 to 12 servings.

A bit of whipped cream to top the dessert adds to the richness.

OPERA SUNDAE

1 can sliced peaches, 1
Number 13 ounce can
2 cups sugar
⅛ teaspoon salt
Juice of 1 lemon and
grated lemon rind
¾ cup maraschino cherry
juice

METHOD:

1. Puree the peaches (put through a sieve).
2. Add the sugar, salt, lemon juice, and cherry juice.
3. Boil 15 minutes and add the grated lemon rind.
4. Serve over ice cream or use as a pudding sauce.

Serves 12-14.

MONACO SUNDAE

1 can Purple Plums (1 lb.
can) (yields 1 cup juice,
1 cup plums)
3 tablespoons cornstarch
¾ cup sugar
¼ teaspoon ground cloves
½ teaspoon ground cinnamon

METHOD:

1. Puree the plums (put through a sieve). Save the juice.
2. Mix the sugar, cornstarch, cloves and cinnamon.
3. Place the juice and pureed plums in the top of a double
   boiler. Add the cornstarch mixture.
4. Cook for 15 minutes.

Serve over ice cream. Top with Whipped Cream.

This may also be used as a pudding sauce.

Serves 12.

PEKINGESE MUFFINS

1 cup sugar
1 cup bread flour, sift before measuring
2 teaspoons baking powder
½ teaspoon salt
1 cup finely chopped pecans
4 well-beaten egg yolks
1 teaspoon vanilla extract
4 stiffly beaten egg whites
2 cups sweetened whipped cream mixed with 3 tablespoons sugar and ½ teaspoon vanilla extract

METHOD:

1. Sift the sugar, flour, baking powder, and salt.
2. Add the pecans and mix together.
3. Add the egg yolks and vanilla extract. Mix.
4. Fold in the egg whites.
5. Bake in well-greased muffin pan. Place a ring of brown wrapping paper in the bottom of each cup. Pour the batter in, filling each cup half full. Bake at 300 F. for 50 minutes.
6. When cool split each muffin into three slices, horizontally, and fill each section with some of the sweetened whipped cream and a dab on the top. Refrigerate until serving.

Yields 12 muffins.

PINEAPPLE STRAWBERRY MERINGUE PUDDING

6 eggs
1 cup sugar
1 cup pastry flour, sift before measuring
1 tablespoon lemon juice
¾ tablespoon grated lemon rind
½ teaspoon vanilla
¼ teaspoon salt
2 cups crushed pineapple
1 cup frozen or fresh strawberries
4 egg whites, stiffly beaten
12 tablespoons sugar
1 teaspoon vinegar

METHOD:

1. Beat the 6 egg whites until stiff and add half the sugar by folding in with long strokes to incorporate air.
2. Beat the 6 egg yolks until light, add the remaining sugar, lemon rind, juice, salt, and vanilla. Beat well.
3. Fold the egg yolk mixture into the egg white mixture. Use care in process to incorporate as much air as possible. Fold the flour in by same method.
4. Pour mixture into a 9 x 13 inch ungreased pan. Bake at 325 F. for 30 to 50 minutes. Remove from oven and spread the pineapple over the top. Next distribute the berries over the top.

5. Beat the 4 egg whites until stiff and add the 12 table-spoons of sugar as you beat. Fold in the vinegar.
6. Spread or place by spoonfulls over the top of the fruit.
7. Bake at 350 F. for 7 minutes.

Yields 20 servings.

PRUNE WALNUT DELIGHT

1 cup cut-up pitted prunes
1½ cups prune juice
2½ cups toasted bread cubes
½ cup brown sugar
½ teaspoon cinnamon
⅛ teaspoon nutmeg
pinch of cloves
¼ cup chopped walnuts
2 tablespoons melted butter

METHOD:

1. Mix together all ingredients except juice.
2. Place in buttered 8 x 8 inch pan.
3. Pour juice over top.
4. Bake at 375 F. for 20 minutes.
5. Serve warm with whipped cream.

Yields 8 servings.

PUMPKINEATER DOUGHNUTS

½ cup sugar
½ teaspoon cinnamon
¼ teaspoon nutmeg
   pinch of cloves
½ teaspoon salt
1 well-beaten egg
2 tablespoons melted butter
½ cup pumpkin, canned
2 cups sifted flour
3 teaspoons baking powder
¼ cup milk
   brown sugar to toss cooked
   doughnuts in

METHOD:

1. Mix sugar with spices and salt.
2. Add beaten egg and mix. Add melted butter.
3. Add pumpkin and mix.
4. Sift the flour with the baking powder and add alternately with the milk.
5. Roll out dough, on a floured pastry board, to ½ inch thickness.
6. Cut into 1½ inch squares and fry in deep fat at 350 F
7. Toss doughnuts into brown sugar to coat well.

You may prefer to toss the doughnuts in powdered sugar.

Yields 4 dozen.

SOUTHERN SHORTCAKE BISCUITS

2 cups flour
3 teaspoons baking powder
⅓ teaspoon baking soda
¼ teaspoon salt
⅓ cup butter or oleo-
margarine
⅓ cup sugar
1 well-beaten egg
1 cup buttermilk

METHOD:

1. Sift the flour, baking powder, salt, and sugar.
2. Work the butter into the flour mixture with the fingertips, as you do for pie crust.
3. Mix the soda with the buttermilk.
4. Add the buttermilk and egg to the flour mixture.
Blend lightly together.
5. Place dough on a floured board and knead lightly.
Roll dough out to ¾ inch thickness. Cut into 2½ inch
rounds and place biscuits on a well-greased baking
sheet. Brush the tops of the biscuits with some melted
butter.
6. Bake at 450 F. for 10 to 12 minutes.

Yields 12 biscuits.

Serve the biscuits warm, split in two and butter between. Place fruit between and also on top of biscuit. Top
with sweetened whipped cream.

The best with fresh strawberries, raspberries, blackberries or peaches. Also very nice as a tea biscuit.

STEAMBOAT PUDDING

    1 cup sugar
    ¼ cup butter
    2 beaten eggs
  1½ cups sifted flour
    ½ teaspoon baking powder
    1 cup buttermilk mixed
      with 1 teaspoon baking
      soda
    ½ cup grated raw carrots
    ¼ cup cut dates
    ¼ cup chopped walnuts

METHOD:

1. Cream butter and sugar.
2. Add the eggs.
3. Sift flour and baking powder.
4. Mix soda and buttermilk and add alternately with the
   flour. Begin and end with some of the flour.
5. Stir in carrots, dates, and nutmeats.
6. Fill 2 well-greased steamer molds or cans half full of
   batter. Cover cans and place in a deep kettle putting
   hot water to cover ½ depth of cans. Cover and boil
   (steam) for 1½ hours.

7. Remove pudding and cut slices thickness desired, about 10-12 to a mold.
8. Serve hot with the following hot sauce.

SAUCE FOR STEAMBOAT PUDDING

2 cups water
1 cup sugar
1 cup butter
4 tablespoons cornstarch
1 cup cold water
2 teaspoons vanilla

METHOD:

1. Place water, sugar, and butter in top of double boiler.
2. Mix cornstarch to a smooth paste with the cold water and add to the sauce. Cook until transparent, stirring often to prevent lumping.
3. Remove from heat and add vanilla.

You may make half a recipe, however, since it requires a steaming process you may wish to save one of the molds for heating up for serving the next day. One mold serves 12 good portions.

NOTES

NOTES

NOTES

Cakes

CHOCOLATE COVERED PEPPERMINT CREAM CAKE

½ cup oleomargarine
1 cup sugar
2 cups sifted cake flour
2½ teaspoons baking powder
¼ teaspoon salt
⅔ cup coffee cream
1 teaspoon peppermint extract
3 stiffly beaten egg whites

METHOD:

1. Blend the sugar and oleomargarine.
2. Sift the flour, baking powder, and salt.
3. Add alternately with the cream, beginning and ending with some of the flour mixture.
4. Add the extract and blend.
5. Fold in the stiffly beaten egg whites.
6. Bake in 2 well-greased layer cake pans at 325 F. for 30 minutes.
7. Cool the cake and fill and frost the cake with the following icing:

3½ cups sifted confectioners' sugar
5 tablespoons cream
¼ cup Dutch process cocoa
1 tablespoon vanilla
¼ cup melted butter

METHOD:

A. Sift the sugar and cocoa together.
B. Add the butter and cream. Whip together until of a creamy consistency. Add the vanilla and blend.
C. Ice the cake.

Serves 12-14.

COCONUT FREDERICK

12 eggs
1 cup sugar
1 cup sifted cake flour
½ cup sugar
1 teaspoon cream of tartar
¼ teaspoon salt
1 teaspoon vanilla

METHOD:

1. Beat egg whites until stiff. Fold in 1 cup of sugar.
2. Sift together flour, ½ cup sugar, cream of tartar, and salt.
3. Beat egg yolks until light and fluffy. Fold into egg whites.
4. Fold in the flour mixture and vanilla.
5. Bake in 3 unbuttered layer cake pans at 350 F. for 30 minutes.
6. Cool. Remove from pans and fill layers with the following filling:

2 cups milk
1½ cups sugar
2 tablespoons cornstarch
2 egg yolks
2 tablespoons butter
2 teaspoons vanilla

METHOD:

1. Beat egg yolks well. Add sugar.
2. Blend cornstarch with the milk and add to the egg mixture.
3. Cook in a double boiler until thickened. Add butter and vanilla.
4. Cool and spread between the cake layers.
5. Ice cake with the following icing:

4 cups whipped cream
½ cup sugar
2 teaspoons vanilla
2 cups grated fresh or short thread coconut
¼ cup cream

METHOD:

1. Blend cream, sugar, and vanilla.
2. Spread over cake.
3. Moisten coconut in ¼ cup cream. Sprinkle over tops and sides of cake.
4. Place cake in refrigerator until serving time.

Serves 16-18.

EDNA'S BIRTHDAY CAKE

2 cups sugar
1 cup shortening
3 beaten egg yolks
1 cup mashed potatoes
1 teaspoon vanilla
1 teaspoon cloves
1 teaspoon cinnamon
¼ teaspoon mace
2 cups sifted cake flour
2½ teaspoons baking powder
½ cup orange juice
3 stiffly beaten egg whites

METHOD:

1. Cream sugar and shortening.
2. Add egg yolks and mix well.
3. Add mashed potatoes.
4. Sift together flour, baking powder, and spices. Add alternately with orange juice.
5. Fold in egg whites.
6. Bake in 2 10 inch layers at 350 F. for 25-30 minutes.
7. Spread filling between layers. (Recipe follows).
8. Frost with boiled icing.

EDNA'S BIRTHDAY CAKE FILLING

2 cups cut-up dates
1 cup sugar
½ cup water
2 beaten egg yolks

METHOD:

1. Mix sugar, water, and dates.
2. Cook slowly to thicken.
3. Add egg yolks.
4. Cook 2 minutes.

Serves 16.

GERMAN LEMON ROLL

6 eggs
1 cup sugar
1 cup cake flour
1 tablespoon lemon juice
¾ tablespoon grated lemon rind
½ teaspoon vanilla
¼ teaspoon salt

FILLING:

2 cups whipped cream
4 tablespoons lemon juice
2 tablespoons grated lemon rind

201

METHOD:

1. Beat egg whites until stiff and add half of the sugar by folding in with long strokes incorporating as much air into the mixture as possible.
2. Beat the yolks until lemon colored, add remaining sugar, lemon rind, juice, salt and vanilla. Beat well.
3. Fold this into the egg whites using long, careful strokes incorporating as much air as possible into the mixture. Fold in the flour by the same method.
4. Place in a 12 x 18 inch cookie pan, ungreased. Bake for 25 minutes at 325 F.
5. Allow to cool for 10 minutes. Turn out onto a piece of wax paper and place a sheet of wax paper over the top. Now roll up as for a jelly roll and twist the ends of the paper to secure the roll together. Allow to cool.
6. Fold the lemon juice and rind into the whipped cream.
7. Unroll the sponge, remove the wax paper and spread the filling over the roll.
8. Again roll the cake up as tightly as possible without breaking it and wrap in wax paper. Place in the refrigerator for 1 hour or longer.
9. Slice and serve with a dash of sweetened whipped cream.

Yields 20 slices.

LADY ELLEN CAKE

¾ cup butter
1½ cups sugar
3 well-beaten egg yolks
1 cup milk
3 cups cake flour, sift before measuring
3¾ teaspoons baking powder
1½ teaspoon vanilla extract
3 egg whites, stiffly beaten
¼ teaspoon yellow food
coloring

METHOD:

1. Cream butter and sugar. Add beaten egg yolks and
blend well.
2. Sift the flour and baking powder and add alternately
with the milk. Begin and end with some of the flour.
3. Add extract and coloring and beat together.
4. Fold in the egg whites.
5. Bake in two 9 inch layer cake pans, well greased, for
30 minutes at 350 F.

Cool and fill with the following filling:

1 cup milk
¾ cup sugar
1 tablespoon cornstarch
1 egg yolk, well beaten
1 tablespoon butter
1 teaspoon vanilla extract

A. Add sugar to the egg yolk.
B. Blend the cornstarch with the milk and add to the egg mixture.
C. Cook mixture in the top of a double boiler, stir to prevent lumping. When mixture thickens add the butter and vanilla.
D. Cool filling. Spread between the cake layers and frost.

ICING:

½ cup cocoa (Dutch process type)
4 cups confectioners' sugar
¼ cup melted butter
6 tablespoons cream
1 teaspoon vanilla extract

METHOD:

1. Sift cocoa and sugar.
2. Add butter, cream, and vanilla.
3. Beat with an electric beater or by hand until icing is creamy and light.
4. Frost top and sides of cake.

You may wish to use a 7 Minute Icing in place of the chocolate icing.

Yields 12 to 16 servings.

PANDORA CAKE

½ cup cocoa dissolved in ½
cup boiling water
¾ teaspoon baking powder
¾ teaspoon baking soda
¾ teaspoon salt
1 cup brown sugar
1 cup white sugar
3 well-beaten eggs
2 cups sifted cake flour
¾ cup buttermilk
1 teaspoon vanilla
¾ cup butter

METHOD:

1. Cream butter and sugars.
2. Add eggs and mix well.
3. Sift flour, baking powder and salt.
4. Mix the baking soda with the buttermilk.
5. Add the flour mixture and the buttermilk alternately, beginning and ending with some of the flour. Mix well.
6. Add the cocoa mixture and mix well. Add vanilla and mix.
7. Bake in 2 layer cake pans at 325 F. for 35-40 minutes.

FILLING FOR PANDORA CAKE

2 eggs, separated
1 cup cooked coffee
1 cup coffee cream
2 tablespoons cornstarch
4 tablespoons flour
½ cup sugar
2 tablespoons vanilla
1 tablespoon butter
1 tablespoon instant coffee

METHOD:

1. Sift sugar, flour, cornstarch and instant coffee.
2. Add liquid coffee and cream and mix well.
3. Cook in top of double boiler to thicken, about 7 minutes.
4. Add beaten egg yolks. Stir well and cook 2 minutes.
5. Add vanilla and butter. Stir and cook 1 minute. Stir the filling as it is cooking. To prevent lumping, use a wire whisk.
6. Cool filling and place between the cake layers.
7. Frost with boiled icing using the two egg whites in the icing. Icing recipe may be found on page 208 in "Cooking with Hougen." This chocolate-coffee cake is rich and very tasty.

Serves 16.

RED RASPBERRY CAKE

½ cup butter
1½ cups sugar
4 eggs, beaten
¾ cup raspberries (use number 303 size can) (drained)
3 cups sifted cake flour
3 teaspoons baking powder
1 teaspoon baking soda
½ teaspoon salt
1 cup of raspberry juice

METHOD:

1. Cream the butter and sugar.
2. Add the beaten eggs and raspberries. Blend well.
3. Sift the flour with the baking powder, soda, and salt.
4. Add the flour mixture alternately with the raspberry juice. Begin and end with some of the flour. Mix well.
5. Bake in 2 well-greased 9 inch layer cake pans at 375 F. for 30 to 40 minutes.
6. While cake is cooling prepare the following filling:

1 cup milk
½ cup sugar
2½ tablespoons flour
⅛ teaspoon salt
2 egg yolks, well beaten (save whites for icing)
1½ teaspoons vanilla

A. Scald milk in top of double boiler.
B. Mix sugar, flour, and salt. Add to milk stirring constantly. Cook until thickened, about 5 minutes.
C. Add egg yolks and cook 3 minutes longer. Add vanilla.
D. Cool. Spread between the 2 layers.

PREPARE THE FOLLOWING ICING

    1 cup red raspberry jam
    1 cup sugar
    ¼ cup water
    2 egg whites

METHOD:

A. Mix sugar and raspberry jam in top of double boiler.
B. Add the water and mix well.
C. Add the egg whites.
D. Place top of boiler over the water bath in bottom of boiler and cook icing. Beat with a rotary beater or electric beater as the mixture cooks. When frosting holds itself in peaks as beater is lifted, about 12 minutes of cooking time, remove icing from fire and stir in ¼ teaspoon of vanilla.
E. Spread on top and sides of cake.

Serves 16.

RIGHT SIDE DOWN SIDE CAKE

1½ cups sugar
¾ cup butter
3 eggs, well beaten
3 cups sifted cake flour
¾ teaspoon nutmeg
¾ teaspoon cloves
¾ teaspoon salt
1½ cups buttermilk
1½ teaspoons soda
1½ cups orange marmalade
1½ cups sliced peaches
¾ cup brown sugar
1½ teaspoons almond extract
1 cup raisins

METHOD:

1. Cream butter and sugar.
2. Add eggs.
3. Sift together flour, nutmeg, cloves, and salt.
4. Mix soda and buttermilk, add to creamed mixture alternately with the flour mixture, beginning and ending with some of the flour.
5. Place remaining ingredients in bottom of greased 9 x 13 inch cake pan.
6. Pour batter on top.
7. Bake at 375 F. for 40 minutes. Turn out upside down. Cut in squares and serve with whipped cream on top.

Serves 18 for dessert, or 12 for dessert and beverage only.

SCHLOSS TORTE

6 eggs
1 cup sugar
1 cup cake flour, sift before measuring
1 tablespoon lemon juice
¾ tablespoon lemon rind, grated
½ teaspoon vanilla
¼ teaspoon salt

METHOD:

1. Beat egg whites until stiff and add half the sugar by folding in with long strokes incorporating as much air into the mixture as possible.
2. Beat the egg yolks until lemon colored, add the remaining sugar, lemon rind, juice, salt, and vanilla. Beat well.
3. Fold this mixture into the egg whites using long careful strokes incorporating as much air as possible. Fold in the flour with the same method.
4. Place the batter in 2 round layer cake pans. Do not grease the pans. Bake for 25 to 30 minutes at 325 F.
5. Allow cake to cool, inverted on a cake cooling rack.

FILLING

1 cup coffee cream
¾ cup sugar
1 tablespoon cornstarch

3 egg yolks, beaten
⅛ teaspoon salt
1 tablespoon butter
1 teaspoon vanilla
3 egg whites
2 tablespoons sugar

METHOD:

A. Place cream in top of a double boiler.
B. Sift sugar, cornstarch, and salt. Add to the cream. Stir with a wire whisk as cooking proceeds to thicken the filling.
C. Add the egg yolks. Stir continuously. Cook 3 minutes. Add the butter and vanilla.
D. Cool filling and place between the cake layers.
E. After torte is filled spread the top with 1 quart of fresh currants, blackberries, or raspberries. If frozen berries are used be sure they are well drained of all moisture.
F. Beat 3 egg whites to a stiff froth and spread over tops of berries. Sprinkle 2 tablespoons of granulated sugar over the egg whites.
G. Place in a 300 F. oven for 15 to 20 minutes. Serve with whipped cream.

The true torte would use fresh currants folded into the egg whites. This gives the topping a look of a cloud with the currants hiding through it.

Serves 16.

SCOTSMAN CAKE

½ cup butter
1 cup sugar
3 well-beaten eggs
2 cups cake flour, sift before measuring
¾ cup chopped fine uncooked oatmeal
½ cup cut fine hazelnuts (filberts)
½ teaspoon salt
½ teaspoon ground cloves
2 teaspoons baking powder
½ teaspoon baking soda
1 cup buttermilk
1 cup apples, chopped fine

METHOD:
1. Blend sugar and butter well. Add the eggs and mix well.
2. Sift the flour with the salt, cloves, and baking powder.
3. Mix the nuts and oatmeal with the sifted flour mixture.
4. Mix the soda and buttermilk together.
5. Add the flour mixture alternately with the buttermilk to the blended sugar and egg mixture. Begin and end with some of the flour. Mix well.
6. Add the chopped apples and blend well.
7. Bake in 2 well-greased 8 inch layer cake pans at 375 F. for 25 minutes.
8. Cool cake and frost and fill the layers with the following icing:

212

ICING:

½ cup oleomargarine
4 cups confectioners' sugar
4 tablespoons cream
½ teaspoon maple extract

METHOD:

1. Whip the softened oleomargarine with an electric beater. Add the sugar, cream, and extract. Beat until light and creamy.
2. Frost between the cake layer and top and sides of cake.

Yields 12-16 servings.

TROPICAL TORTE

4 egg whites, beaten stiff but moist
½ cup confectioners' sugar
3 egg yolks, well beaten
½ cup cake flour, sift before measuring
⅛ teaspoon salt
½ teaspoon vanilla

METHOD:

1. Add sugar gradually to the egg whites as you beat.
2. Add egg yolks and vanilla by folding in method.

3. Sift flour and salt. Add by folding in.
4. Place a piece of unbuttered brown paper on a cookie pan.
5. Spread batter over top of paper. Dust top with confectioners' sugar. Bake 15 minutes at 350 F.
6. Remove from paper by carefully rolling paper edge down.
7. Prepare filling while cake is baking.

FILLING:

> ½ pound dried apricots
> ½ cup sugar
> 2 firm ripe bananas, cut into cubes

METHOD:

1. Wash apricots, soak in boiling hot water for ½ hour.
2. Drain and cover with water to top of apricots. Cook until soft.
3. Add sugar.
4. Rub apricot mixture through a sieve.
5. Add bananas. Cool mixture.
6. Cut cake layer into 3 parts. Place filling between each layer. Sprinkle top layer with confectioners' sugar. Cut into slices and serve with whipped cream.

Serves 16 to 18.

NOTES

NOTES

Pies

APPLE AND ORANGE PIE

¼ cup butter
1 quart sliced green apples
2 cups sugar
1 tablespoon cinnamon
1 pint orange sections
1 unbaked pie shell and rolled top crust (for 9 inch pie)

METHOD:

1. Mix the cinnamon and sugar together.
2. Mix apples with cinnamon sugar.
3. Place a layer of apples in the pie shell.
4. Place a layer of the orange sections over the apples.
5. Place remaining apples over the orange sections.
6. Dot bits of the butter over the top of apples.
7. Place rolled top crust over the apples. Prick a few holes in the top of the crust with the tines of a fork.

Bake at 375 F. until tender, about 45 minutes.

A nine inch pie should cut 8 servings.

CAPE CRANBERRY PIE

1 unbaked pie shell and 1 top crust (9 inch size crust)
1½ cups sugar
1 teaspoon cinnamon
1 tablespoon flour
¼ teaspoon salt
1 cup orange juice
3 cups fresh or frozen cranberries
2 well-beaten eggs
2 tablespoons melted butter

METHOD:

1. Combine the sugar, cinnamon, salt, orange juice, and flour. Mix to smooth ingredients. Place in the top of a double boiler and cook to thicken mixture, about 5 minutes. Stir to prevent lumping.
2. Remove from the heat and add the berries, butter, and eggs.
3. Place in the pie shell and top with the other crust.
4. Bake at 400 F. for 40 minutes.

Yields 1 nine inch pie serving 8 to 10.

CHERRY PIE, BILLY BOY

2 cans No. 303 size 1 lb of sour pitted cherries
1½ cups cherry juice, drained from the cherries
1½ cups sugar
3½ tablespoons cornstarch
¼ teaspoon salt
2 tablespoons butter
½ teaspoon almond extract
1½ tablespoons sugar for top of pie
1 unbaked pie shell and 1 top crust, 9 inch size

METHOD:

1. Drain juice from the cherries and measure out 1½ cups juice.
2. Sift sugar, salt, and cornstarch and mix with the juice.
3. Place mixture in the top of a double boiler and cook for 5 minutes to thicken. Stir to prevent sticking.
4. Add the butter and extract. Remove from the heat. Add the cherries.
5. Pour the mixture into the pie shell and top with the other pie crust. Sprinkle the top with the 1½ tablespoons of sugar.
6. Bake at 400 F. for 45 minutes.

Yields one 9 inch pie serving 8 to 10 pieces.

HOT PRUNE PIE WITH LEMON SAUCE

1 unbaked pie shell and extra dough for lattice top crust
1½ pounds dried prunes
¾ cup grape juice
1½ tablespoons cornstarch
6 tablespoons orange juice
10 tablespoons sugar
⅛ teaspoon salt
juice of 1 lemon
2 egg yolks, well beaten
2 tablespoons butter
Use a 9 inch pie pan

METHOD:

1. Simmer the prunes with the grape juice and 2 cups of water. They should be cooked 20 minutes.
2. Pit the prunes. 2 cups of prunes are needed.
3. Mix 1 cup of the prune juice with the cornstarch, sugar, salt, lemon juice, and orange juice. Cook in the top of a double boiler until transparent and slightly thickened. Stir.
4. Add the egg yolk. Stir and cook 3 minutes.
5. Remove from the stove and add the prunes. Pour into the unbaked pie shell. Dot the top with the butter, cut in bits.
6. Roll the remaining pie dough and cut strips ½ inch wide and form a lattice work top crust for the pie.

7. Bake at 375 F. for 45 minutes.
8. Serve with hot lemon sauce.

LEMON SAUCE

¾ cup sugar
2 cups water
3 tablespoons cornstarch
¼ cup lemon juice
grated rind of 1 lemon
¼ cup butter

METHOD:

A. Mix sugar and cornstarch.
B. Place water in top of double boiler and add the sugar mixture. Cook until thickened and transparent.
C. Add the butter, lemon juice, and rind.
D. Serve hot over the warm pie.

Serves 10.

HUCKLEBERRY FINN PIE

1 can of blackberries in heavy syrup (15 oz. size)
1 can blueberries in heavy syrup (15 oz. size)
4 tablespoons cornstarch
1 cup sugar
¼ teaspoon salt
2 tablespoons butter
2 tablespoons lemon juice
1 9 inch pie shell and top crust (rolled out)

METHOD:

1. Drain the juice from the berries.
2. Sift the next 3 ingredients, add the juice mixing to make a smooth combination.
3. Place in the top of a double boiler and cook, stirring to prevent lumping, for 15 minutes.
4. Remove from the fire and add the lemon juice and butter.
5. Fold in the berries. Place in the unbaked pie shell.
6. Top the berries with the rolled top crust. Cut a few slits in the top crust to allow the steam to escape.
7. Bake at 400 F. for 40 minutes.

A 9 inch pie serves 8 to 10.

LEMON MERINGUE PIE

1 baked pie shell
5 tablespoons cornstarch
¼ teaspoon salt
1 cup sugar
3 cups water
¾ cup lemon juice (fresh)
4 beaten egg yolks
½ cup butter
4 stiffly beaten egg whites
12 tablespoons sugar
1 teaspoon grated lemon rind
1 teaspoon vinegar

METHOD:

1. Mix cornstarch, sugar, and salt.
2. Add water and lemon juice. Cook slowly in the top of a double boiler until thickened, approximately 10 minutes. Stir to prevent lumping.
3. Add the well-beaten egg yolks and cook 5 minutes. Stir to prevent lumping.
4. Remove from the fire and add the butter. Mix.
5. Place filling in the baked pie shell. When cooled somewhat spread the top with a meringue made as follows:
   A. Fold the sugar into the stiffly beaten egg whites by beating as you gradually add the sugar.
   B. Add the lemon rind and the vinegar and beat until meringue stands in peaks.
6. Bake at 375 F. for 12 minutes.

Yields one 9 inch pie.

MARSHALL HOUSE MINCEMEAT PIE

1 unbaked pie shell and rolled crust to form lattice top
¼ cup butter
½ cup sugar
¼ cup molasses (sorghum molasses or dark Karo syrup)
½ teaspoon salt
1 egg
2 cups mincemeat
½ to ¾ cup chopped pecans
2 tablespoons grated orange rind
½ cup orange juice
1½ apples cut in cubes
Use 9 inch pie pan

METHOD:

1. Cream butter and sugar together.
2. Add molasses, salt, and beaten egg. Beat well.
3. Add mincemeat, pecans, apples, orange juice and rind.
4. Mix well together.
5. Place in pie shell and top with strips of crust cut ⅜ inch wide to form a lattice work top.
6. Brush top with cream. Bake at 400 F. for 30 to 40 minutes.
7. Serve with Hard Sauce.

Serves 8 portions.

NEW ORLEANS COFFEE PIE

 1 tablespoon plain gelatin
¼ cup cold water
 3 tablespoons cornstarch
¾ cup sugar
¼ teaspoon salt
⅛ teaspoon nutmeg
2½ cups brewed coffee
 3 teaspoons instant coffee (freeze dried)
 3 well-beaten egg yolks
 3 well-beaten egg whites, light and fluffy
 1 cup whipped cream
 1 teaspoon rum extract
 1 tablespoon vanilla extract
½ cup grated sweet chocolate
 1 baked pie shell, 9 inch shell

METHOD:

1. Sprinkle the gelatin over the cold water.
2. Sift the cornstarch, sugar, salt, and nutmeg.
3. Dissolve the freeze dried coffee in the hot liquid coffee. Add the cornstarch mixture to the coffee and blend well. Place in the top of a double boiler and cook until thickened, about 10 minutes. Stir with a wire whisk to prevent lumping.

4. Add the egg yolks and stir as you cook for 3 minutes.
5. Remove from the heat and add the gelatin and mix well.
6. Cool this mixture until it has the constancy of whipped cream. Add the extracts. Fold in the whipped cream.
7. Fold in the egg whites and pile the mixture into the pie shell.
8. Top with the grated chocolate. Refrigerate the pie for 2 hours.

Serve with a dopple of whipped cream on top of each serving of pie.

Yields 8 to 10 servings.

OLD SOUTH PEACH PIE

2 nine inch unbaked pie
shells, one for top crust
2 eggs
½ teaspoon almond extract
¼ cup butter
½ cup sugar
1 tablespoon cornstarch
3 cups sliced canned
peaches, drained, use No.
2½ size can
½ cup chopped pecans

METHOD:

1. Blend cornstarch and sugar. Add the peach juice and stir to blend smoothly.
2. Cook in the top of a double boiler for 5 minutes to thicken the mixture. Add the beaten egg and cook for 3 minutes.
3. Add the peaches, pecans, butter, and extract. Blend.
4. Place mixture in pie shell and top with top crust.
5. Bake at 400 F. for 45 minutes.

Serves 8 to 10.

PIE CRUST

2 cups flour
¾ teaspoon baking powder
½ teaspoon salt
⅔ cup lard
4 tablespoons cold water

METHOD:

1. Sift flour before measuring. Sift again with salt and baking powder.
2. Work the lard into the flour using the finger tips.
3. Add the water and mix. Divide the dough into 2 parts.
4. Place on a floured pastry board and roll out the pie crust.

Yields 2 nine inch pie crusts.

RAISIN PIE

1 tablespoon cornstarch
2 cups orange juice
¼ cup lemon juice
1 cup sugar
2 cups seedless raisins
2 well-beaten eggs
2 tablespoons butter
¼ teaspoon cinnamon
⅛ teaspoon ground cloves
pinch of salt
2 tablespoons grated orange rind
2 pie crusts, one for the bottom crust and one for the top.

METHOD:

1. Mix the cornstarch with the orange juice to form a smooth paste.
2. Add the lemon juice and sugar. Place in the top of a double boiler. Cook four minutes, stir to prevent lumping.
3. Mix the other ingredients into the hot sauce. Pour the mixture into an unbaked pie shell. Top with the other unbaked pie crust.
4. Bake at 400 F. for 40 minutes.

Yields one 9 inch pie.

Serves 8-10.

231

NOTES

NOTES

NOTES

INDEX

BREAKFAST DISHES

SOUPS

MEATS, POULTRY, AND ACCOMPANIMENTS

VEGETABLES AND POTATOES

SALADS

BREADS AND ROLLS

COOKIES AND PUNCHES

DESSERTS

CAKES

NOTES

NOTES

NOTES

NOTES

NOTES

NOTES

NOTES